DATE DUE   JUL 03

GAYLORD			PRINTED IN U.S.A.

Step-by-Step Dollmaking

Barbara Marsten

Technical Writing by Christine Makowski

Illustrations by Tina Bliss

Photography by René Velez

VNR VAN NOSTRAND REINHOLD COMPANY
New York   Cincinnati   Toronto   London   Melbourne

To my family who inspired me
and to Pierre and Valentin for having faith that I could do it.

Acknowledgments

I am grateful to Barry Nathan for suggesting that I write this book and for bringing me to Van Nostrand Reinhold. Thank you to Nancy Green for help in shaping the book and to Susan Rosenthal Gies who has been ever helpful and wise in her editing.

Also special thanks to Christine Makowski for writing clear and easy-to-follow instructions, to Tina Bliss for her charming and beautiful illustrations, to René Velez for his beautiful photographs.

Thank you to Nora O'Leary at *Family Circle* and to Cecilia Toth at *Good Housekeeping* for permission to include projects that were featured in their magazines.

Printed in the United States of America
Designed by Jean Callan King/Visuality

Published by Van Nostrand Reinhold Company
A division of Litton Educational Publishing, Inc.
135 West 50th Street, New York, NY 10020, U.S.A.

Van Nostrand Reinhold Limited
1410 Birchmount Road
Scarborough, Ontario M1P 2E7, Canada

Van Nostrand Reinhold Australia Pty. Ltd.
17 Queen Street
Mitcham, Victoria 3132, Australia

Van Nostrand Reinhold Company Limited
Molly Millars Lane
Wokingham, Berkshire, England

16 15 14 13 12 11 10 9 8 7 6 5 4 3 2 1

Library of Congress Cataloging in Publication Data

Marsten, Barbara.
  Step-by-step dollmaking.
  Includes index.
  1. Dollmaking. 2. Textile crafts. I. Makowski, Christine. II. Title.
TT175.M37   745.592'21   80-14752
ISBN 0-442-25139-4   AACR1

Contents

Metric Conversion Table

Linear Measure

1 inch = 2.54 centimeters
12 inches = 1 foot = 0.3048 meter
3 feet = 1 yard = 0.9144 meter

Square Measure

1 square inch = 6.452 square centimeters
144 square inches = 1 square foot = 929.03 square centimeters
9 square feet = 1 square yard = 0.8361 square meter

Introduction

Ever since I was a small child I have been creating my own dolls and stuffed animals. Now, as a doll and toy designer, I want to show you how to make thirty dolls and animals from simple, easy-to-follow patterns and instructions.

The projects I've included in this book require no special tools—just a sewing machine—no special skills—just a basic knowledge of sewing—and no special materials. Construction methods for all of the dolls are simple, and instructions are step-by-step and fully illustrated. All patterns are printed full size and may be traced directly from the pages of the book.

Rag dolls and stuffed animals are loved by boys as well as girls, and, because of their stylized look (and for nostalgic reasons too) adults enjoy them immensely. You will find quite a variety of dolls on the following pages. All are made completely of cloth, and all fabrics and trims are readily available. There are a series of male and female costume dolls, each one depicting a region of the United States; a trio of men, each employed in a different occupation; a rag doll family; a group of plump animals; six humorous dolls scaled to dollhouse size; lion and tiger toys with their own lion tamer; several pillow-dolls, including a French sailor, a cupid, and a flying angel; a lovely pajama-bag doll for a little girl's room; and a set of whimsical pot-holder dolls to dress up your kitchen. All of the dolls' hairdos are completely made of fabric—either flat felt or puffy yo-yo's like the ones in your grandmother's quilts. It is this element and the stylization and simplicity of the designs that make these dolls unique and so much fun to do.

The projects range from the simple Engineer to the more time-consuming Rag Doll Family, but only a beginner's knowledge is required to make any of them. In fact, you might even use these projects to help you teach your children how to sew. They will benefit from and love the step-by-step, illustrated approach.

Dollmaking is an exciting pastime. You'll be cutting and stitching along, when suddenly, you're adding two circles for the eyes. Magically, your doll comes alive with a personality of its own. You've created a character. I hope you enjoy these dolls as much as I do and continue to enjoy them for years to come.

CHAPTER 1

General Notes on Dollmaking

I have included this chapter in order to help you make these dolls in the most efficient way. Before beginning your first project, read over the following notes. You'll learn about the tools needed, marking and cutting the fabric, sewing, stuffing, and assembling the dolls, and some general hints that will make your work easier.

Tools You Will Need

Basically, if you do any sewing at all, you already have most of the tools you will need to make any of the dolls in this book. Because it can be very frustrating to have to stop your work to hunt for scissors or straight pins every time you come to a new step, it's a good idea to assemble all your tools and materials in one place, such as a work basket or desk drawer.

The following is a list of essential tools:

- Scissors, large or medium size, for cutting cloth and patterns
- Scissors, small and curved, for cutting features
- Blunt dowels, in a variety of sizes, for turning and stuffing
- White glue, for gluing hands and features
- Tracing paper, for making patterns
- Needles, sharps for sewing; crewels for embroidering
- Straight pins
- Thimble
- Pencil
- Tailor's chalk or light pink or peach-colored pencil for marking cloth
- Small safety pin, for threading elastic or ribbons
- Sewing machine
- Tape measure
- Ruler
- Brown wrapping paper (optional), for making heavier-duty patterns
- Cardboard, for patterns of pieces to be used numerous times

Making the Patterns

The patterns for each doll—the body parts, features, and articles of clothing—are all together in the back of the book starting on page 97. You will be tracing each part directly from the book. A good seamstress knows the importance of a neat, accurate pattern, so it's important that you learn how to do this step well.

To trace the patterns you will simply place the tracing paper directly over the pattern in the book and trace over the lines. Use masking tape to hold the paper in place while you are tracing and use a sharp-pointed pencil to trace the lines; make all lines clear and crisp. Be sure to include lines for darts, tucks, gathers, etc., and all lines that appear on the pattern. Copy down all labels too, such as the name of the pattern part (arm, eye, pantalettes, etc.) and the number of each piece to be cut.

If you plan to make more than one of the particular doll you are working on, it's probably a good idea to use a heavy brown wrapping paper or construction paper for the patterns so that they will hold up to repeated use. In this case, make your tracing paper patterns the same way. Then, trace around them onto heavier paper. For pattern pieces such as yo-yo's and bow ties, in other words, for pieces that you will be using repeatedly within one project alone, I recommend that you transfer your traced pattern onto heavy cardboard.

All pattern pieces in the book are shown full size. You will not have to enlarge pieces on a graph before you begin to trace. Where it is not necessary to show the whole item, half of the pattern piece is given, the folded side indicated. When tracing these patterns, draw them exactly as they are shown in the book, drawing in the center foldline. Since tracing paper is transparent, you may then turn over the paper and, matching the center foldline, trace the other half, completing the pattern.

Some of the larger body pattern pieces are shown in two sections on the pattern pages. They are either extended across two pages or both pieces are on one page. These are clearly noted on the patterns with lettered arrowheads marked "join" on the edges to be joined. Trace these patterns up to and including the joining line, and then trace the other part of the pattern, matching joining lines. (Look for asterisks.)

For each doll the pattern pieces are listed with the directions. Some pattern pieces are simply rectangles or squares, the dimensions of which are given. Make a paper pattern for each of these to complete your set of patterns.

Marking and Cutting the Fabric

Your next step is, of course, to mark and cut the fabric. Iron out all wrinkles before you begin and find yourself a big, empty space to work upon.

Place the fabric so that the grainline follows the direction of the foldlines on the pattern. All rectangular or square pieces follow the straight of grain, so they are not cut on the bias. The smaller pattern pieces are to be placed on the fabric and traced around while held in place. Use dressmaker's pencil, tailor's chalk, or a light-colored pencil to trace. I use a pale peach or pink-colored pencil for dark and light fabrics alike. When working with larger pattern pieces, pin in several places so that cutting will be accurate.

Mark all darts and pleats before you remove pattern with tailor's chalk or a pink-colored pencil. Don't use pens for marking. If a pencil mark shows, it can always be washed off later with a little soap and water.

To mark the features of the dolls' faces, place a dot at the centers of the eyes and noses. When the doll is finished, this will serve as a guide for placement. Use a thin pink line for the mouth. I backstitch over this line with embroidery thread before I embroider the mouth. This helps keep the embroidery stitches even. If you are using felt for the mouth, glue it over a thin line marking the placement. If you'd rather place the features on the finished dolls where they seem most attractive to *you*, eliminate the guide markings I've included on the patterns.

For dolls with white felt faces and hands, use two layers of felt, as indicated. This way, faces will be opaque and hands will be sturdy.

Cut out all pieces along the marked lines. Cut all notches outward, adding extra fabric, rather than cutting into seam allowances. Be sure to cut all notches shown, so you will have no trouble assembling dolls. A curved nail scissors is helpful too for cutting small, rounded features accurately.

Tips on Fabrics and Notions

The fabric and notions listed are readily available in fabric shops, department stores, and variety stores.

Here are some tips to keep in mind regarding materials:

- Felt fabrics are available in many weights. I have used a 50% wool felt which is a medium-weight felt of good quality.
- Felt fabric is specified for pieces of the dolls that are not hemmed, because felt does not fray or ravel. Please do not substitute other fabrics for felt.
- Unless another weight is suggested, always use medium-weight fabric.
- No-iron fabrics, such as blends of polyester and cotton, won't wrinkle and give a neat appearance to the dolls. However, for small, tightly stuffed pieces, such as the arms and legs of the Rag Doll Family, polyester/cotton blends ravel too easily and will fray at the seams. Here I used 100% cotton.
- If flesh-colored fabric is not available for some of the dolls that list it as required, use unbleached muslin or tint muslin with dye or tea.
- These toys are not meant to be washable. If you wish to be able to wash the Rag Doll Family, make hair of color-fast polyester and cotton and use color-fast embroidery threads for eyes, cheeks, and mouth. Stuff these dolls with washable stuffing.
- Use flame-retardant fabrics if possible for bedside dolls for children.
- If fabric has a nap, stripes, or one-way pattern, be sure to allow for extra yardage so that pattern pieces can be cut correctly.
- All lace and eyelet trims called for are white.
- Use any scraps of laces, rickracks, edgings, and ribbons you have on hand if the colors are right and if they are similar to the widths and styles suggested.
- A beautiful polyester double-face satin ribbon only ⅛ inch wide is manufactured in a large variety of colors by C. M. Offray and Son, Inc. (address: C. M. Offray & Sons, Inc., 261 Madison Ave., New York, N.Y. 10016). It is wonderfully suitable to dollmaking.
- For self-gripping closing of the Pajama-Bag Doll use a product such as "Velcro®" Brand self-gripping fasteners.
- The miniature and full-size buttons that I have used are readily available in notions departments, variety stores, or button shops.
- I have specified long pipe cleaners for the inside of the rabbit and pig ears. However, if one pipe cleaner is not long enough, join two together.
- Use flexible white glue such as Slomon's Sobo

glue or Elmer's Glue-All for all gluing. Do not use rubber cement as it bleeds through the cloth.

- I generally use polyester fiber filling for stuffing. It is springier than cotton, is relatively inexpensive, and is easily found in a variety of stores. If you wish, you may also use kapok or cotton batting.
- For stitching use cotton-covered polyester, or #50 cotton sewing thread. Use thread that matches fabrics, unless contrasting thread is indicated in the instructions.
- For embroidered features, use six-strand embroidery floss in the thickness specified in directions.
- For mouths of Women dolls a snip of narrow red rickrack in the form of a V can be substituted for felt, or you might embroider the mouths with red embroidery thread.

If you plan to present a young child with one of these dolls, it's a good idea to follow this checklist:

- Obtain the manual prepared by the U.S. Consumer Product Safety Commission, Washington, D.C. 20207 and follow its advice concerning safety in the manufacture of toys for children.
- Make sure that all fabrics used are dye-fast.
- Use fire-retardant fabrics wherever possible.
- Use only new fabrics and stuffing, not recycled goods.
- Use stuffing which is nonallergenic. Do not use kapok.
- Double-sew all seams so that no stuffing will come out.
- Instead of using buttons for eyes and trim, use felt circles, sewn or glued on securely. If you do use buttons, use only one-piece construction buttons, and sew them on very securely.
- Be sure that you have removed all pins.
- Test all glued-on pieces to make sure that they cannot be removed.
- Do not use pipe cleaners or any items that could be detached and swallowed.

Sewing the Dolls

Here are some tips to help you sew your dolls. Keep in mind that these dolls were designed to be sewn by machine, but any of the steps could be done by hand.

- Use ¼-inch seam allowances on all projects unless otherwise indicated.
- Use small machine stitches when sewing on small pieces of fabric. I use approximately 12 to 15 stitches to the inch.
- Be sure to backstitch at the beginning and end of all seams sewn by machine.
- Remove all basting threads after each step is sewn by hand or machine. If basting threads are not removed before next step, they may be difficult to remove.
- To close openings on dolls after turning, use a tiny hidden slipstitch.
- You may wish to reinforce inward curves by stitching over curves a second time.
- Trim seam allowances, as shown in the instructions, after sewing. Clip all inward curves to help in turning and so seam allowances will lay flat inside finished doll. Be sure not to clip through your stitches or the seam will open.
- When working with small pieces of fabrics, I generally baste rather than use pins.
- Machine-gather with the longest stitch available on your sewing machine.
- When embroidering features on dolls or animals, be sure not to pull threads too tightly.
- Be sure to use matching thread when sewing felt faces and when sewing mustaches and sideburns to face so stitches will not be seen.
- Sew trims of gold braid or laces onto dolls by hand with a tiny invisible running stitch so that no machine-stitch line shows.

Assembling the Dolls

Assembling the dolls is most important in determining their finished look. Remember, the placement of the facial features and hair creates the personality of your doll, so check their expressions before gluing or sewing on the features.

- Stuff dolls tightly, as they will loosen slightly in time. However, don't fill arms and legs to the top or they will be difficult to join to the body.
- When using polyester fiber filling, pull out the stuffing to make it fluffier and to keep it free from lumps.
- Small pieces must be filled by pushing stuffing, small bits at a time, into them. Push stuffing very tightly into hands and corners. You can use any dowel with a rounded end, such as a knitting nee-

dle, a pencil with the point broken off and the end rounded, a long-pointed wooden paintbrush handle, or a chopstick for this purpose.

- Stuff small spaces, such as hands, thumbs, and corners, first.
- After stuffing, mold toy to its desired shape by squeezing and patting it.
- Let glue dry thoroughly before assembling any glued pieces.
- If you are making more than one doll at a time, save time by using an assembly-line construction technique. First, assemble all materials. Then trace all patterns. Next, cut all pieces; then sew all pieces needing the same color thread, etc. Clip, turn, and stuff dolls as a group.
- After turning pieces to right side, and before stuffing, run a knitting needle or rounded dowel along the inside of the seamlines to open out the spaces fully.
- When gluing on facial features, use a very small amount of glue so that it will not bleed through the feature. If this happens, you can glue on another layer of the feature right over the stained one to hide the stain.

CHAPTER 2

Three American Couples

It was my fascination with American folk art and Americana in general that led me to design these three couples. Each one represents a particular region in America's history—Daniel Boone and his bride, Tina, the Frontier Girl; Colonel Max and his wife, Mimi, the belle from the Old South; and Captain Wooly and his wife, Christine, from New England. All are dressed in stylized versions of period costumes.

The simple construction is the most distinguishing feature of these six dolls. Faces, hair, arms, shoes, and costume trim are sewn to the unassembled front and back body pieces, which are then sewn together to form a pillowlike doll with unstuffed arms and legs. The dolls range in size from 15 to 16 inches in height. Finally, hats, skirts, and other finishing touches are added. The finished dolls seem much more elaborate than they actually are.

Pattern Pieces (see pages 104 through 112)

BODY (2), SLEEVE (2), TUNIC (1), NECK FRINGE (1) from BODY fabric
CAP (2), TAIL (1) from fur CAP fabric
FACE (2), HAND (4) from FACE fabric
BOOT (2), BELT (2), EYE (2) from BOOT fabric
MUSTACHE (1), SIDEBURN (2), HAIR BACK (1) from HAIR fabric

Materials Required

BODY fabric, ¼ yard of artificial buckskin
CAP fabric, 9 by 14 inches of fake fur
FACE fabric, 9 by 10 inches of white felt
BOOT fabric, 9 by 6 inches of black felt
HAIR fabric, 9 by 6 inches of chestnut brown felt
Stuffing, polyester fiber filling

Making the Doll

Cut out all pieces.

STEP 1. MAKING THE BODY FRONT

A. Baste the two layers of FACE together, with the raw edges even. Pin the face to the right side of one BODY section at the dotted line position on the pattern, and stitch close to the outer edges.

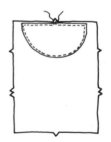

B. Baste SIDEBURNS and MUSTACHE to the face, as shown in the drawing, and stitch in place close to the outer edges.

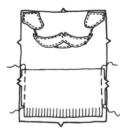

Daniel Boone
the Frontiersman

Brave Daniel Boone is from Frontier Country. He is made of artificial buckskin, a synthetic fabric similar to suede that does not ravel, and wears a fake coonskin cap. Whatever fabric you choose for Daniel, make sure that it will not ravel where the fringe is cut.

When cutting the fake fur for Daniel's hat, put the top of the pattern piece at the top of the nap so that the fur runs downward and is fluffy at the top of the face. Cut fake fur from the back by sliding scissors into the base of the nap to avoid cutting off fur. When stitching, if any fur gets caught, pick it out with a needle or pointed tool.

C. Cut 1-inch slashes in lower edge of TUNIC, as shown on pattern, spacing them ¼ inch apart to form fringe. Baste the tunic to the right side of body front, matching the double notches.

D. Baste BELT to the right side of body front, covering the upper edge of the tunic. Machine-stitch close to the long edges of belt.

E. Cut 1½-inch slashes in lower edge of NECK FRINGE, as shown on pattern, spacing them ¼ inch apart. Stitch a tiny dart at center of neck fringe, as shown in the drawing. Baste fringe to right side of body front touching the edges of the face, with the point ½ inch below center of face. Machine-stitch neck fringe along upper edge.

F. Stitch one CAP section to the upper edge of body front, with right sides facing, matching the notches and making sure fur is tucked away from stitching.

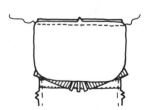

STEP 2. MAKING THE SLEEVES AND BOOTS

A. Cut along solid lines of each SLEEVE as shown on pattern, to form fringe. Glue two layers of each HAND together. Baste the hand to the right side of each sleeve, matching the notches.

B. Fold the sleeves in half, with right sides facing, and stitch the short, straight end. Turn the sleeve right side out, baste the raw edges to meet fringe, as shown, and press, using a press cloth. Machine-stitch along the long edge at fringe. Baste the sleeves to the right side of body front, matching the notches and making sure the neck fringe is free.

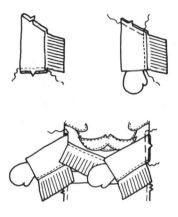

C. Baste BOOTS to the right side of the lower edge of body front, with the edges ¼ inch apart at center. Stitch boots in place.

STEP 3. MAKING THE BODY BACK

A. Baste HAIR BACK to the right side of remaining BODY section, matching the notches and with the raw edges even.

B. Stitch remaining CAP section to the upper edge of the body back, with the right sides facing and matching the notches.

C. Baste remaining BELT section to the right side of body back, at the same level as belt on front. Stitch close to the long edges of belt.

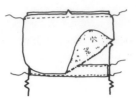

STEP 4. ASSEMBLING THE BODY

A. Baste the body back to the body front, with right sides facing. Stitch, making sure fur is tucked away from stitching, and keeping the sleeves, boots, fringe, and tunic fringe tucked into the body, leaving an opening at bottom.

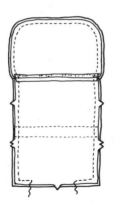

B. Turn the body right side out. Stuff it firmly and sew the opening closed.

C. Glue EYES to face, as shown in the drawing.

D. Sew TAIL to left side of cap.

The Frontier Girl

Tina, Daniel Boone's bride, is an American country girl. She is wearing a black calico dress and bonnet with a red pin-dot apron and white eyelet pantalettes. Choose any calico print for the dress and a stripe, pin-dot, or solid fabric for the apron.

Pattern Pieces (see pages 98 through 103)

BODY (2), SLEEVE (2), SKIRT RUFFLE (1) cut a rectangular pattern 3½ by 26 inches, HAT (1), BRIM (2+1 Interfacing), TIES (2) cut a rectangular pattern 1 by 10½ inches, HAT BINDING (1) cut a rectangular pattern 1½ by 7 inches, from BODY fabric
APRON (1), POCKET (4) from APRON fabric
FACE (2), HAND (4) from FACE fabric
SHOE (2), EYE (2) from SHOE fabric
HAIR FRONT (1), HAIR BACK (1) from HAIR fabric
CHEEK (2) from CHEEK fabric
MOUTH (1) from MOUTH fabric
PANTALETTE (2) from eyelet edging
BRIM (1) from interfacing

Materials Required

BODY fabric, ½ yard of calico print fabric
APRON fabric, 9 by 10 inches of red pin-dot fabric
FACE fabric, 9 by 6 inches of white felt
SHOE fabric, 9 by 3 inches of black felt
HAIR fabric, 7 by 14 inches of brown felt
CHEEK fabric, bright pink felt scrap
MOUTH fabric, red felt scrap
PANTALETTE fabric, ⅜ yard of 3⅛-inch-wide eyelet edging
Interfacing fabric, 9 by 4 inches of pellon
Bow for hair, ⅜ yard of ⅜-inch-wide red velvet ribbon
Stuffing, polyester fiber filling

Making the Doll

Cut out all pieces.

STEP 1. MAKING THE BODY FRONT AND BACK

A. Baste the two layers of FACE together, with the raw edges even. Pin the face to the right side of one BODY section at the solid line position on the pattern, and stitch close to the outer edges.

B. Baste HAIR FRONT to the body front, right sides up, matching the notches and with the raw edges even.

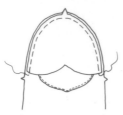

C. Baste HAIR BACK to the right side of the remaining BODY section, matching the notches and with raw edges even. Tie a bow from a 10-inch length of ribbon. Trim ends diagonally. Attach bow to bottom of hair back, catching body back with a few stitches, as shown in the drawing.

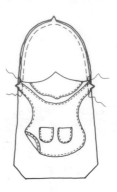

STEP 2. MAKING THE APRON

A. Turn under ¼ inch on neck and outer edges of APRON. Stitch close to the turned edges.

B. Pin POCKET sections together, with right sides facing. Stitch, leaving an opening. Turn the pocket right side out, sew the opening closed, and press. Pin pockets to the right side of the apron, as shown in the drawing, and stitch close to the sides and lower edges.

C. Baste the apron to the body front, with the right sides up and matching the notches.

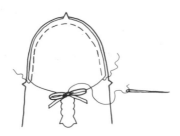

STEP 3. MAKING THE SLEEVES AND LEGS

A. Glue two layers of each HAND together. With right sides together, baste a hand to each SLEEVE, matching the notches.

B. Fold each sleeve in half, with right sides facing. Stitch, leaving the slanted edge open. Turn the sleeves right side out, baste the raw edges together, and press. With right sides up, baste the sleeves to the body front, matching the notches.

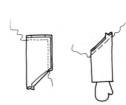 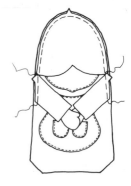

16

C. Fold each PANTALETTE in half, with right sides facing and notches matching, and stitch the short side. Turn right side out.

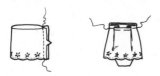

D. Insert SHOE in pantalette, placing the pantalette seam at the center back of the shoe. Make two small pleats at the upper edge, following the arrows on pattern. Baste pleats in place through all layers. With right sides together, baste the pantalettes to the lower edge of the body, leaving a ½-inch space between shoe tops. Stitch pantalettes in place.

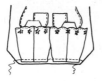

STEP 4. ASSEMBLING THE BODY

A. Baste the body back to the body front, with right sides facing. Stitch, keeping the sleeves and shoes tucked into the body and leaving an opening at bottom.

B. Turn the body right side out. Stuff the body firmly and sew the opening closed.

STEP 5. MAKING THE RUFFLE

A. For the SKIRT RUFFLE, use the rectangle 3½ inches long and 26 inches wide. Turn under ¼ inch on long edges and machine-stitch. Fold the SKIRT RUFFLE in half, with right sides facing, and stich the short side. Turn right side out.

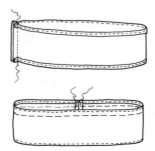

B. By machine, stitch a gathering stitch along the upper edge of the skirt ruffle. Place it on the doll, 3 inches up from the bottom, with the seam at the center back. Pull the gathers and adjust them evenly. Knot the gathering threads securely. Remove the skirt ruffle carefully, and stitch over gathers with small stitch by machine to hold them in place. Place skirt ruffle on doll and sew securely in place by hand.

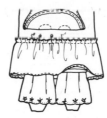

STEP 6. FINISHING THE DOLL

A. Glue EYES, CHEEKS, and MOUTH to the face, as shown in the drawing.

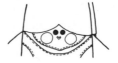

B. Run a machine gathering stitch along all edges of HAT.

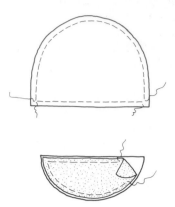

C. Baste interfacing to one BRIM section. Pin the two brims together, with right sides facing, and stitch along the curved edge. Turn the brim right side out and press. Pin one layer of brim to the straight edge of the hat, with right sides facing. Pull up the gathers of hat to fit and adjust them evenly. Stitch and press the seam allowances toward brim. Turn in the free edge of the brim and sew it in place over the seam.

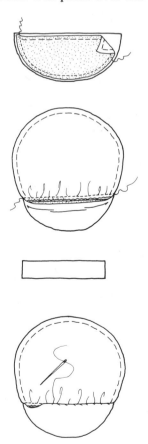

D. For HAT BINDING, use the rectangle 1½ by 7 inches. Pin the hat binding to the curved back edge of the hat, turning in the short ends ¼ inch. Pull up gathers to fit and adjust them evenly. Stitch and press the seam allowances toward the binding. Fold the binding in half and sew the free edge in place over the seam and across the ends.

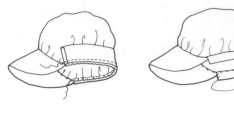

E. For TIES, use the two rectangles each 1 by 10½ inches. Turn under ¼ inch on all edges. Fold the ties in half lengthwise and stitch the turned edges together. Sew ties securely to ends of hat binding. Place hat on the doll and tie at front.

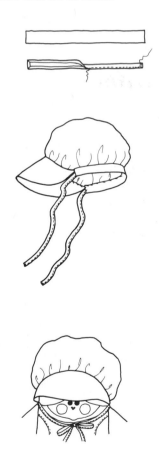

The Southern Colonel

Our Southern gentleman, Colonel Max, is dashing in his steel gray menswear uniform and hat. He is trimmed with six brass buttons, a brass belt buckle, and gold braid. Use cotton, wool, or any gray fabric suitable for a Southern uniform. If you'd prefer to make a Northern soldier, use navy blue for his uniform and leave off the goatee.

Pattern Pieces (see pages 105 through 112)

BODY (2), SLEEVE (2), JACKET (2), BRIM (2+1 Interfacing), from BODY fabric
FACE (2), HAND (4) from FACE fabric
BOOT (2), BELT FRONT RIGHT (1), BELT FRONT LEFT (1), BELT BACK (1), EYE (2) from BOOT fabric
MUSTACHE (1), GOATEE (1), SIDEBURN (2), HAIR BACK (1) from HAIR fabric

Materials Required

BODY fabric, ½ yard of gray menswear
FACE fabric, 9 by 8 inches of white felt
BOOT fabric, 9 by 10 inches of black felt
HAIR fabric, 9 by 4 inches of chestnut brown felt
Interfacing fabric, 10 by 7 inches of pellon
Jacket trim, ⅓ yard of ¼-inch-wide gold braid
Belt buckle, 1- or 1¼-inch-wide brass buckle
Jacket buttons, six ½-inch brass buttons
Stuffing, polyester fiber filling

Making the Doll

Cut out all pieces.

STEP 1. MAKING THE BODY FRONT

A. Baste the two layers of FACE together, with the raw edges even. Pin the face to the right side of one BODY section at the dotted line position on the pattern and stitch close to the outer edges.

B. Baste SIDEBURNS, GOATEE, and MUSTACHE to the face, as shown in the drawing, and stitch in place close to the outer edges.

STEP 2. MAKING THE JACKET AND BELT

A. Fold JACKET pieces along the foldline, with right sides facing and double notches matching. Stitch along the lower edge. Turn jacket pieces right side out, baste raw edges, and press. Baste the jacket pieces to the right side of body front, matching the double notches. Machine-stitch along the upper edge.

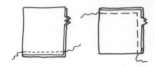

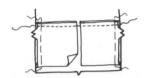

B. Baste RIGHT and LEFT BELT FRONT to the right side of body front, covering the upper edge of the jacket. Slip right belt through buckle, turning back 1½ inches on end. Sew in place. Buckle left belt, as shown in the drawing.

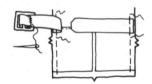

STEP 3. MAKING THE SLEEVES AND BOOTS

A. Sew gold braid by hand to position shown on each SLEEVE pattern, forming a point at the center, as shown in the drawing. Glue two layers of each HAND together. Baste the hands to the right side of each sleeve, matching the notches.

B. Fold the sleeve in half, with right sides facing and the hand inside. Stitch, leaving the slanted edge open. Turn each sleeve right side out, baste the raw edges

together, and press. Baste the sleeves to the right side of body front, matching the single notches.

 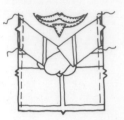

C. Baste BOOTS to the right side of the lower edge of the body front, with the edges ¼ inch apart at center. Stitch boots in place.

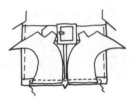

STEP 4. MAKING THE BODY BACK

A. Baste HAIR BACK to the right side of remaining BODY section at the dotted line position. Machine-stitch close to the long edges.

B. Baste BELT BACK to the right side of body back at the same level as belt on front.

STEP 5. ASSEMBLING THE BODY

A. Baste body front to body back, with right sides facing. Stitch, keeping the sleeves, boots, and jacket tucked into body and leaving an opening at bottom.

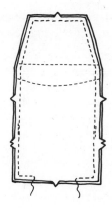

B. Turn the body right side out. Stuff it firmly and sew the opening closed.

C. Glue EYES to face, as shown in the drawing. Sew six brass buttons to jacket front, as shown in the drawing.

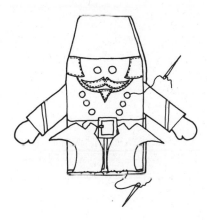

STEP 6. MAKING THE HAT BRIM

A. Baste interfacing to wrong side of one BRIM section. Stitch the ends of the brim, matching the notches, and press seam open. Pin the brim sections together, with right sides facing, and stitch the outer edges.

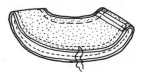

B. Turn the brim right side out and press. Turn under ¼ inch on inner curved edges of brim, and stitch together. Place brim over head. Sew the brim in place along the brim seam. Turn up the right side of brim and tack in place to body.

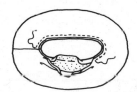

The Southern Belle

Our beautiful belle, Mimi, has coppery curls under her pink felt hat. Her matching dress has three rows of ruffles, plus there are ruffles on her sleeves, and the hat and dress are trimmed with pink velvet ribbon. You could use pastel cotton or a tiny floral print for Mimi's dress. Mimi carries a nosegay of tiny velvet artificial flowers, which are available among the trims in your fabric shop. Her pantalettes are embroidered eyelet, which also surrounds the nosegay.

Pattern Pieces (see pages 99 through 103)

BODY (2), SLEEVE (2), SKIRT (2), SKIRT RUFFLE (3) cut a rectangular pattern 3½ by 36 inches, SLEEVE RUFFLE (2) cut a rectangular pattern 2¾ by 8 inches, NOSEGAY HOLDER (1) from BODY fabric
HAT FRONT (1), HAT BACK (1), BRIM (1) from HAT fabric
FACE (2), HAND (4) from FACE fabric
SHOE (2), EYE (2) from SHOE fabric
HAIR FRONT (1), HAIR BACK (1), CURL (3) from HAIR fabric
CHEEK (2) from CHEEK fabric
MOUTH (1) from MOUTH fabric
PANTALETTE (2) from eyelet edging

Materials Required

BODY fabric, ¾ yard of pink or floral print cotton
HAT fabric, 9 by 18 inches of pink felt
FACE fabric, 9 by 6 inches of white felt
SHOE fabric, 9 by 3 inches of black felt
HAIR fabric, 9 by 18 inches of coppery-colored felt
CHEEK fabric, bright pink felt scrap
MOUTH fabric, red felt scrap
PANTALETTE fabric, ⅜ yard of 3⅛-inch-wide eyelet edging
NOSEGAY HOLDER trim, ½ yard of ¼-inch pale blue velvet ribbon and ½ yard of 1½-inch-wide eyelet edging
NOSEGAY, tiny artificial flowers
Dress trim, 1¼ yards of ¼-inch-wide pink velvet ribbon
Stuffing, polyester fiber filling

Making the Doll

Cut out all pieces.

STEP 1. MAKING THE BODY FRONT AND BACK

A. Baste the two layers of FACE together, with the raw edges even. Pin the face to the right side of one BODY section at the solid line position on the pattern, and stitch close to the outer edges.

B. Baste HAIR FRONT to the right side of body front, matching the notches and with the raw edges even. Baste HAT FRONT to the right side of hair front, matching the notches and with the raw edges even.

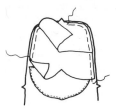

C. Baste HAIR BACK to the right side of the remaining BODY section, matching the notches and with the raw edges even. Baste HAT BACK to the right side of hair back, matching the notches and with the raw edges even.

STEP 2. MAKING THE SLEEVES AND SHOES

A. Glue the two layers of each HAND together. Baste a hand to the right side of each SLEEVE, matching the notches.

B. Fold the sleeve in half, with right sides facing. Stitch, leaving the slanted edge open. Turn the sleeve right side out, baste the raw edges together, and press.

C. For SLEEVE RUFFLES, use the two rectangles each 2¾ by 8 inches. Turn under ¼ inch on the long edges and machine-stitch. Fold the ruffle, with right sides facing, and stitch the short sides together. Turn right side out. Run a gathering stitch ½ inch from the upper edge. Place the ruffle on the sleeve, overlapping the hand ½ inch. Pull up the gathers and adjust them evenly. Knot the gathering threads securely and baste. Then sew the ruffle in place by machine. Cover gathering threads with ribbon and sew in place.

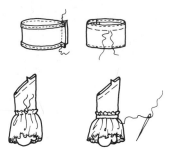

D. Baste the sleeves to the right side of body front, matching the notches.

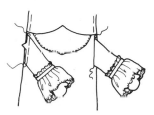

E. Fold PANTALETTE, with right sides facing, notches matching, and stitch the short side. Turn right side out.

F. Insert SHOE inside pantalettes, with the pantalette seam at the center back on the shoe. Make two pleats at the front upper edge, following arrows on the pattern. Baste pleats in place through all layers. Baste the shoes to the right side of lower edge of body, leaving a ½-inch space between shoe tops. Stitch shoes in place.

 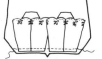

STEP 3. ASSEMBLING THE BODY

A. Baste the body back to the body front, with the right sides facing. Stitch, keeping the sleeves and shoes tucked into the body and leaving an opening at bottom.

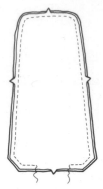

B. Turn the body right side out. Stuff the body firmly and sew the opening closed.

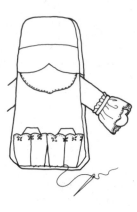

STEP 4. MAKING THE SKIRT

A. Turn upper and lower edges of SKIRT under ¼ inch and machine-stitch. Pin skirt sections together, with right sides facing, and stitch the sides. Turn right side out.

B. For skirt ruffles, use the three rectangles each 3½ inches long and 36 inches wide. Turn long edges under ¼ inch and machine-stitch. Fold the ruffle, with

right sides facing, and stitch the short sides together. Turn right side out. Run a gathering stitch ½ inch from the upper edge.

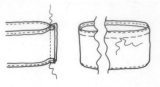

C. Starting at the bottom, pin the ruffles to the skirt, at the lower edge, pinning at the center and along the top edge, with right sides up and with the seams at one side. Pull up gathers and adjust them evenly. Knot the gathering threads securely. Baste and then sew ruffles to skirt by machine.

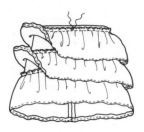

D. Place the skirt on the doll and sew it securely in place. Cover the gathering threads on the upper ruffle with ribbon and sew in place.

STEP 5. FINISHING THE DOLL

A. Glue EYES, CHEEKS, and MOUTH to the face, as shown in the drawing.

B. Place BRIM over the hat, with the raw edges even at front. Lift up the front brim and sew it in place by hand between body seams. Turn down the front brim. Tie a piece of ribbon into a small bow and sew it to the back brim.

C. Starting at the bottom, wrap CURL around a pencil and sew the ends securely in place. Sew curls to right side of head under hat brim, as shown in the drawing.

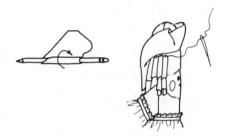

D. Turn the curved edge of NOSEGAY HOLDER under ¼ inch and machine-stitch. Fold nosegay holder, with right sides facing, and stitch the straight edge. Turn right side out. Sew eyelet ruffling to the open end of nosegay.

E. Insert tiny artificial flowers inside nosegay holder and sew them in place. Tie a ribbon into a bow and sew to nosegay holder. Sew nosegay holder securely to left hand.

The New England Sea Captain

Captain Wooly from New England wears a navy blue cotton uniform trimmed with gold braid. Gray flannel felt or gray wool flannel should be used for his beard. If you use flannel instead of felt, add ¼-inch seam allowances all around the beard pattern and turn back ¼-inch hems so that the flannel will not ravel; and, if you'd rather make a younger sea captain, use chestnut brown for the beard instead of gray. The six nautical brass buttons on his uniform are readily available in notions departments.

Pattern Pieces (see pages 104 through 110)

BODY (2), SLEEVE (2), JACKET (1), HAT FRONT (1), HAT TOP (1) from BODY fabric
FACE (2), HAND (4) from FACE fabric
VISOR (1), BOOT (2), EYE (2) from BOOT fabric
BEARD (1) from BEARD fabric
NOSE (1) from NOSE fabric

Materials Required

BODY fabric, ⅜ yard of navy blue cotton, cotton duck, canvas, denim, or wool flannel
FACE fabric, 9 by 10 inches of white felt
BOOT fabric, 9 by 7 inches of black felt
BEARD fabric, 7 by 6 inches of gray wool flannel or gray flannel felt
NOSE fabric, red felt scrap
Hat and Jacket trim, ½ yard of ½-inch-wide gold braid
Jacket buttons, six ¾-inch nautical brass buttons
Stuffing, polyester fiber filling

Making the Doll

Cut out all pieces.

STEP 1. MAKING THE BODY FRONT

A. Baste the two layers of FACE together, with the raw edges even. Pin the face to the right side of one BODY section at the dotted line position on the pattern, and stitch close to the outer edges.

B. Baste BEARD to face, with the upper raw edges even. If using woven fabric, add and turn in ¼-inch seam allowances all around and machine-stitch.

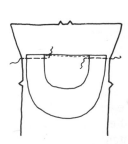

26

C. Turn under ¼ inch on lower straight edge of HAT FRONT and baste. Make small pleats at sides of hat front, as shown in the drawing, and baste them in place.

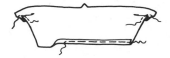

D. Pin the curved edge of HAT TOP to the upper edge of hat front, with right sides facing and matching the single notches. Stitch the curved seam. Turn right side out. Baste the hat to body front; place the lower basted edge ¼ inch over face and beard, matching double notches and with the raw edges even. Stitch close to the lower edge of hat.

E. Pin VISOR ½ inch above lower edge of hat and stitch close to the straight edge. Pin gold braid to hat front, covering the upper edge of visor. Sew the braid in place by hand.

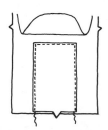

F. Turn upper and side edges of JACKET under ¼ inch and baste. Baste the jacket to the right side of body front, matching the center notches and with the raw edges even. Stitch close to the sides and upper edge of jacket.

STEP 2. MAKING THE SLEEVES AND BOOTS

A. Sew gold braid by hand ½ inch above lower edge of each SLEEVE. Glue two layers of each HAND together. Baste a hand to the right side of each sleeve, matching the notches.

B. Fold each sleeve in half, with right sides facing and hand inside. Stitch, leaving the slanted edge open. Turn each sleeve right side out, baste the raw edges together, and press. Baste each sleeve to the right side of body front, matching the notches.

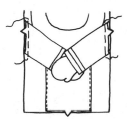

C. Baste BOOTS to the right side of the lower edge of body front, with the edges ¼ inch apart at center. Stitch boots in place.

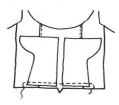

STEP 3. ASSEMBLING THE BODY

A. Baste the remaining BODY section to the body front, with right sides facing. Stitch, keeping the sleeves, boots, and hat top tucked into the body and leaving an opening at bottom.

B. Turn the body right side out. Stuff it firmly and sew the opening closed.

C. Glue EYES and NOSE to the face.

D. Sew six buttons to jacket.

The Sea Captain's Wife

Christine, Captain Wooly's wife, is made of bright red cotton fabric. She could be made of any cotton in a solid, pinstripe, pin-dot, or tiny print, or in a cotton or wool flannel, or in a small-scale wool print. Her hair is dark brown felt, but for an older version, you might use gray flannel felt.

Pattern Pieces (see pages 98 through 102)

BODY (2), SLEEVE (2), SKIRT (2) from BODY fabric
HAT (2), APRON (2), WAISTBAND and TIE (3), PANTA-
    LETTES (2) from HAT fabric
FACE (2), HAND (4) from FACE fabric
SHOE (2), EYE (2) from SHOE fabric
HAIR FRONT (1), HAIR BUN (1) from HAIR fabric
CHEEK (2) from CHEEK fabric
MOUTH (1) from MOUTH fabric

Materials Required

BODY fabric, ⅜ yard of bright red cotton, cotton or
    wool flannel, or wool
HAT fabric, ⅜ yard of white batiste
FACE fabric, 9 by 6 inches of white felt
SHOE fabric, 9 by 3 inches of black felt
HAIR fabric, 9 by 6 inches of dark brown felt
CHEEK fabric, bright pink felt scrap
MOUTH fabric, red felt scrap
Dress trim, ¾ yard of ½-inch-wide edging
Apron and pantalette trim, 1 yard of ¼-inch-wide edg-
    ing
Hat trim, 1¼ yards of ⅜-inch-wide navy blue ribbon
Stuffing, polyester fiber filling

Making the Doll

Cut out all pieces.

STEP 1. MAKING THE BODY FRONT AND BACK

A. Baste the two layers of FACE together, with the raw edges even. Pin the face to the right side of one BODY section at the solid line position on the pattern, and stitch close to the outer edges.

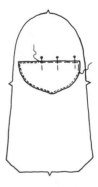

28

B. Baste HAIR FRONT to the right side of the body front, matching the notches and with the raw edges even.

C. Pin HAIR BUN to the right side of remaining BODY section at the dotted line position. Stitch around top of bun.

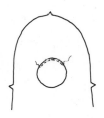

STEP 2. MAKING THE SLEEVES AND SHOES

A. Sew ¼-inch-wide edging by hand, ¾ inch above lower edge of each SLEEVE. Glue the two layers of each HAND together. Baste the hands to the right side of each sleeve, matching the notches.

B. Fold the sleeve in half, with right sides facing and hand inside. Stitch, leaving the slanted edge open. Turn the sleeve right side out, baste the raw edges together, and press. Baste the sleeves to the right side of body front, matching the notches.

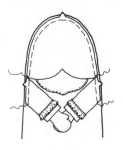

C. Turn under ¼ inch on bottom edge of each PANTALETTE and machine-stitch. Pin ¼-inch-wide edging to the right side of lower edge and sew in place. Fold each pantalette, with right sides facing and notches matching, and stitch the short side. Turn right side out.

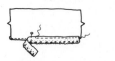

D. Insert a SHOE inside each pantalette, with the seam at the center back of each shoe. Make two pleats at the front upper edge, following arrows on the pattern. Baste pleats in place through all layers. Baste the shoes to the right side of lower edge of the body, leaving a ½-inch space between shoe tops. Stitch shoes in place.

 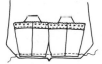

STEP 3. ASSEMBLING THE BODY

A. Baste the body back to the body front, with right sides facing. Stitch, keeping the sleeves and shoes tucked into the body and leaving an opening at bottom.

B. Turn the body right side out. Stuff it firmly and sew the opening closed.

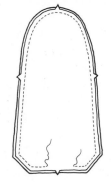 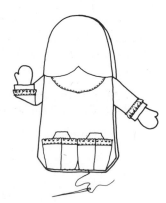

STEP 4. MAKING THE SKIRT AND THE APRON

A. Turn under ¼ inch on the lower edge of each SKIRT section and machine-stitch. Sew ½ inch-wide edging by hand ½ inch above lower edge of the skirt. Pin skirt sections together, with right sides facing, and stitch up from the lower edge to the notches. Turn under ¼ inch on upper and side edges and machine-stitch.

B. Place the skirt on the doll, matching the side seams. Make two pleats at the upper edges, following the arrows on the pattern, and baste. Sew skirt securely to body by hand through all layers.

C. Pin APRON sections together, with right sides facing. Stitch along the sides and lower edge and turn the apron right side out. Make two pleats at the upper edge, following the arrows on pattern, and baste. Sew ½-inch-wide edging by hand to the lower edge of apron.

D. Center and pin apron to one edge of WAISTBAND; then stitch. Press seam allowances toward waistband.

E. Turn under ¼ inch on long edges and one short edge of each TIE, and machine-stitch. Make a pleat at the raw end so it measures ¾ inch and baste. Baste pleated end of each tie to end of waistband. Turn the waistband to inside, turning in ¼ inch on all edges. Stitch along ends and lower edge.

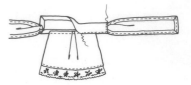

F. Put apron on doll and tie in back. Secure apron in place at sides with tiny stitches.

STEP 5. FINISHING THE DOLL

A. Glue EYES, CHEEKS, and MOUTH to the face.

B. Pin HAT sections together with right sides facing. Stitch, leaving an opening. Turn hat right side out, sew the opening closed, and press. Run a gathering stitch 1 inch all around edges of hat.

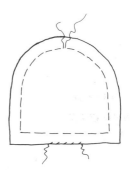

C. Place the hat on the doll, with the straight edge at the back. Pull up the gathers and adjust them evenly. Remove hat and machine-stitch gathers securely in place. Place ribbon over this row of stitching, covering gathering threads, and sew in place with tiny stitches. Make two tiny bows of ribbon and stitch into place at front of hat.

CHAPTER 3

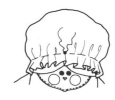

Three Working Men

These three working men—Ben the Engineer, Peter the Policeman, and Louis the Lion Tamer—are extremely easy to make. They are constructed in the same manner as the Three American Couples and the French Sailor pillow-doll (see page 94). First, all pieces of trim, face, arms, and boots are sewn to the front of the doll. Then the finished doll front is sewn to the doll back, forming a simple rectangular doll, or pillow, with unstuffed arms and legs. Any of these dolls could easily be adapted to accessories for a child's bedroom, and could set a red, white, and blue decorative color scheme. All three dolls are approximately 18 inches tall.

Pattern Pieces (see pages 104 through 112)

Pattern Pieces (see pages 104 through 112)

BODY (2), SLEEVE (2), BIB (1) from BODY fabric
KERCHIEF (1) from KERCHIEF fabric
FACE (2) from FACE fabric
BOOT (2), MUSTACHE (1), SIDEBURN (2), EYE (2) from
 BOOT fabric
HAND (4), VISOR (1) from HAND fabric

Materials Required

BODY fabric, ⅜ yard of navy blue and white mattress
 ticking or striped denim
KERCHIEF fabric, 5 by 5 inches of red bandana fabric
FACE fabric, 9 by 7 inches of white felt
BOOT fabric, 9 by 6 inches of black felt
HAND fabric, 9 by 7 inches of red felt
Overall buttons, two ¾-inch brass buttons
Stuffing, polyester fiber filling

Making the Doll

Cut out all pieces.

The Engineer

Our stalwart Engineer, Ben, is one of the first toys that
I ever designed. Extremely simple to make, he can be
made with navy and white mattress ticking or striped
denim. He is stitched in black to accent his overalls,
his buttons are brass, and he sports a real bandana in
his overall pocket.

STEP 1. MAKING THE BODY FRONT

A. Baste the two layers of FACE together, with the
raw edges even. Pin the face to the right side of one
BODY section at the dotted line position on the pattern, and stitch close to the outer edges.

B. Baste SIDEBURNS and MUSTACHE to the face, as shown in the drawing, and stitch in place close to the outer edges.

C. Baste VISOR ½ inch above the face and stitch close to the straight edge.

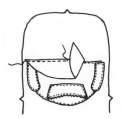

D. Turn under ¼ inch on upper and curved edges of BIB. Machine-stitch along the curved edges. Baste bib to the right side of body front, matching the center notches. Stitch bib in place along the upper edge and down the center, as shown in the drawing.

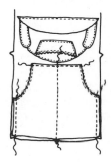

STEP 2. MAKING THE SLEEVES AND BOOTS

A. Glue two layers of each HAND together. Baste a hand to the right side of each SLEEVE, matching the notches.

B. Fold each sleeve in half, with right sides facing, and with hand inside. Stitch, leaving the slanted edge open. Turn the sleeve right side out, baste the raw

edges together, and press. Baste the sleeves to the right side of body front, matching the notches.

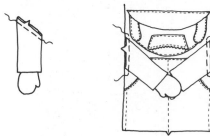

C. Baste BOOTS to the right side of the lower edge of body front, with the edges ¼ inch apart at center. Stitch boots in place.

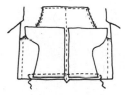

STEP 3. ASSEMBLING THE BODY

A. Baste the remaining BODY section to the body front, with right sides facing. Stitch, keeping the sleeves and boots tucked into the body and leaving an opening at bottom.

B. Turn the body right side out. Stuff it firmly and sew the opening closed.

C. Glue EYES to face, as shown in the drawing. Sew buttons to upper corners of bib.

D. Turn in ¼ inch on all edges of KERCHIEF. Turn in ¼ inch again and machine-stitch. Stuff kerchief in bib pocket.

The Policeman

Peter the Policeman is made of navy cotton fabric. He is trimmed with gold braid, and eight brass buttons embossed with the American Eagle march up and down his jacket front. He will guard your house well!

Pattern Pieces (see pages 105 through 112)

BODY (2), SLEEVE (2), JACKET (1), BRIM (2) from BODY fabric
FACE (2), HAND (4) from FACE fabric
BOOT (2), MUSTACHE (1), SIDEBURN (2), EYE (2) from BOOT fabric

Materials Required

BODY fabric, ⅜ yard of navy blue cotton
FACE fabric, 9 by 8 inches of white felt
BOOT fabric, 9 by 6 inches of black felt
Hat trim, ¼ yard of ½-inch-wide gold braid
Jacket trim, ¾ yard of ¼-inch-wide gold braid
Jacket buttons, eight ¾-inch brass buttons
Stuffing, polyester fiber filling

Making the Doll

Cut out all pieces.

STEP 1. MAKING THE BODY FRONT

A. Baste the two layers of FACE together, with the raw edges even. Pin the face to the right side of one BODY section at the dotted line position on the pattern, and stitch close to the outer edges.

B. Baste SIDEBURNS and MUSTACHE to the face and stitch in place close to the outer edges.

C. Pin BRIM sections together, with the right sides facing. Stitch, leaving the long, straight edge open. Turn the brim right side out, baste the raw edges together, and press. Baste the brim ½ inch above face, and machine-stitch close to the straight edge.

D. Baste ½-inch-wide gold braid to the body front, covering the raw edge of the brim. Sew the braid in place by hand.

E. Turn under ¼ inch on upper and side edges of JACKET and baste. Baste the jacket to the right side of body front, matching the center notches, with the raw edges even. (Top of jacket overlaps chin slightly.) Stitch close to the sides and upper edges of jacket.

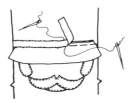

STEP 2. MAKING THE SLEEVES AND BOOTS

A. Sew a piece of ¼-inch-wide gold braid by hand to the lower edge of each SLEEVE, ½ inch above edge. Sew another piece 1 inch above edge. Glue two layers of each HAND together. Baste a hand to the right side of each sleeve, matching the notches.

B. Fold each sleeve in half, with the right sides facing and with the hand inside. Stitch, leaving the slanted edge open. Turn each sleeve right side out, baste the raw edges together, and press. Baste the sleeves to the right side of body front, matching the notches.

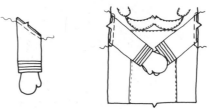

C. Baste BOOTS to the right side of the lower edge of body front, with the edges ¼ inch apart at center. Stitch boots in place.

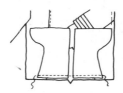

STEP 3. ASSEMBLING THE BODY

A. Baste the remaining BODY section to the body front, with the right sides facing. Stitch, keeping the sleeves and boots tucked into the body and leaving an opening at the bottom.

B. Turn the body right side out. Stuff it firmly and sew the opening closed.

C. Glue EYES to the face, as shown in the drawing.

D. Sew eight buttons to jacket.

The Lion Tamer

Louis the Lion Tamer is a very handsome fellow. Louis is made of bright red velveteen (but any bright solid color cotton, velveteen, wool flannel, or pinwale corduroy will work nicely), and is trimmed with gold braid and a plethora of brass buttons. Louis has worked hard to train Maurice the Tiger and Leon the Lion (see pages 65 through 68) so that they will make excellent pets. The three make wonderful accessories for a child's room.

(see pages 65 through 68)

Pattern Pieces (see pages 119 through 120)

BODY (2), SLEEVE (2), JACKET (1) from BODY fabric
FACE (2), HAND (4) from FACE fabric
BOOT (2), FRINGE (3), VISOR (1), EYE (2) from BOOT fabric
MUSTACHE (1), SIDEBURN (2) from MUSTACHE fabric

Materials Required

BODY fabric, ⅜ yard of bright red velveteen, cotton, wool flannel, or pinwale corduroy
FACE fabric, 9 by 8 inches of white felt
BOOT fabric, 9 by 10 inches of black felt
HAIR fabric, 3 by 5 inches of chestnut brown felt
Epaulette and Hat trim, ½ yard of ½-inch-wide gold braid
Jacket trim, 1¼ yards of ¼-inch-wide gold braid
Jacket buttons, ten ½-inch brass buttons
Hat button, one ¾-inch brass button
Stuffing, polyester fiber filling

Making the Doll

Cut out all pieces.

STEP 1. MAKING THE BODY FRONT

A. Baste the two layers of FACE together, with the raw edges even. Pin the face to the right side of one BODY section at the dotted line position on the pattern, and stitch close to the outer edges.

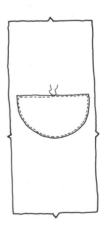

B. Baste SIDEBURNS and MUSTACHE to face, as shown in the drawing, and stitch in place close to the outer edges.

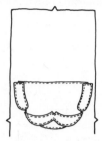

C. Cut along solid lines of FRINGE pattern. Pin one fringe to body, with the fringed edge upward and lower point touching face at center. Baste in place.

D. Pin VISOR ½ inch above face, covering edge of fringe point. Stitch close to the straight edge.

E. Pin ½-inch-wide gold braid to the body front, covering the edge of the visor and point of the fringe. Sew the braid in place by hand.

STEP 2. MAKING THE JACKET

A. Turn under ¼ inch on upper and side edges of JACKET and baste. Baste the jacket to the right side of body front, with the raw edges even and matching the center notches. Stitch close to the sides and upper edges of the jacket.

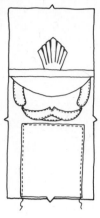

B. Cut five lengths of ¼-inch-wide gold braid, each 5½ inches long. Pin this braid to jacket, ¾ inch apart, turning in ends to form loops, as shown in the drawing. Sew the braid in place between the loops.

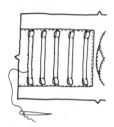

STEP 3. MAKING THE SLEEVES AND BOOTS

A. By hand, sew ¼-inch-wide gold braid ½ inch above lower edge of each SLEEVE. Glue two layers of each HAND together. Baste a hand to the right side of sleeve, matching the notches.

B. Pin a FRINGE to each sleeve, with the pointed raw edges even, and baste. Sew ½-inch-wide gold braid to the upper edge of each sleeve, at the dotted position on pattern, as shown in the drawing.

C. Fold each sleeve in half, with right sides facing and with hand inside. Stitch, leaving the slanted edge open. Turn the sleeve right side out, baste the raw edges together, and press. Baste the sleeves to the right side of the body front, matching the notches.

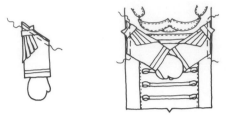

D. Baste BOOTS to the right side of the lower edge of body front, with the edges ¼ inch apart at center. Stitch boots in place.

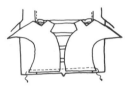

STEP 4. ASSEMBLING THE BODY

A. Baste the remaining BODY section to the body front, with the right sides facing. Stitch, keeping the sleeves and boots tucked into the body and leaving an opening at bottom.

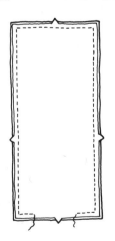

B. Turn the body right side out. Stuff it firmly and sew the opening closed.

C. Glue EYES to the face, as shown in the drawing.

D. Sew ten small gold buttons to ends of jacket braid and one large gold button to center of braid above visor.

CHAPTER 4

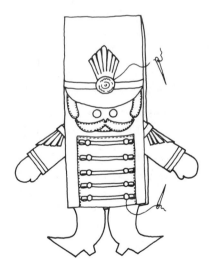

Six Miniatures

Here is a group of miniature dolls, 5 to 6 inches tall, each of which can be made entirely of scraps. Scaled to fit for dollhouses or miniature collections, the group includes a captain and his wife, a fisherman wearing a yellow slicker, two Civil War soldiers—one from the North and one from the South—and a Southern belle. All are made of a variety of cotton fabrics and felts.

If you wish, you can fill these miniature dolls with dried flowers or a potpourri so that you can use them as sachets. They are also just the right size to hang as ornaments on a Christmas tree.

The Miniature Sea Captain

Simon the Sea Captain is a salty old New England sailor. He is made of navy blue cotton and trimmed with gold braid and small gold buttons with embossed anchors. The brim of his hat is black felt and his beard is gray flannel felt.

Pattern Pieces (see pages 113 through 114)

BODY (2), SLEEVE (2), COAT (2) from BODY fabric
BOOT (2), BOOT TOP (2), VISOR (1), EYE (2) from BOOT fabric
FACE (1), HAND (2) from FACE fabric
BEARD (1) from BEARD fabric
NOSE (1) from NOSE fabric

Materials Required

BODY fabric, 9 by 14 inches of navy blue cotton
BOOT fabric, 9 by 5 inches of black felt
FACE fabric, 2 by 4 inches of white felt
BEARD fabric, 3 by 3 inches of gray flannel felt
NOSE fabric, red felt scrap
Coat and Hat trim, ⅓ yard of ⅜-inch-wide gold braid
Coat buttons, four ¼- to ½-inch nautical gold buttons
Stuffing, polyester fiber filling

Making the Doll

Cut out all pieces.

STEP 1. MAKING THE BODY FRONT

A. Baste FACE to the right side of one BODY section at the dotted line position, as shown on pattern, and stitch close to the outer edges.

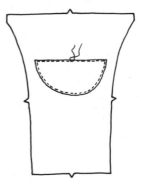

B. Glue BEARD to the face, with upper raw edges even and leaving bottom free.

C. Pin VISOR ¼ inch above edge of face, and stitch close to the straight edge, by hand.

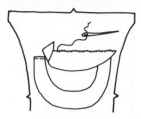

STEP 2. MAKING THE SLEEVES AND BOOTS

A. By hand, sew gold braid ⅜ inch above lower edge of each SLEEVE. Baste a HAND to the right side of each sleeve, matching the notches.

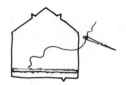

B. Fold each sleeve in half, with right sides facing. Stitch, leaving the slanted edge open. Turn the sleeve right side out, baste the raw edges together, and press. Baste the sleeves to the right side of body front, matching the notches.

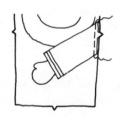

C. Fold each BOOT, as shown in the drawing, and stitch from A to B. Turn boot right side out. Fold extension over boot and stitch across fold, forming heel.

D. Stitch the long seam on each BOOT TOP. Turn right side out, bringing the seam to the center back. Slip the extension of the boot into the bottom of the boot top, and sew together by hand.

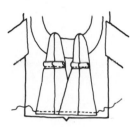

E. Baste boots to the right side of the lower edge of body front, with the edges overlapping at center, as shown. Stitch boots in place.

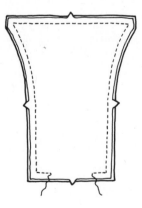

STEP 3. ASSEMBLING THE BODY

A. Baste the remaining BODY section to the body front, with right sides facing. Stitch, keeping the sleeves and boots tucked into the body and leaving an opening at bottom.

B. Turn body right side out. Stuff it firmly to within 1 inch of boot tops. Baste and stitch 1 inch from boot tops to hold stuffing in place. Sew the bottom opening closed by hand.

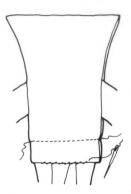

STEP 4. MAKING THE JACKET

A. Pin COAT sections together, with right sides facing. Stitch, leaving an opening. Turn right side out, press, and sew the opening closed by hand.

B. Wrap coat around body, overlapping at right side of doll, and sew in place by hand. Sew four brass buttons to coat, as shown in the drawing.

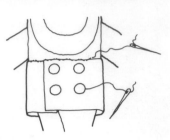

STEP 5. FINISHING THE DOLL

A. Glue EYES and NOSE to the face, as shown in the drawing.

B. Sew gold braid over the straight edge of visor and along the back, as shown in the drawing.

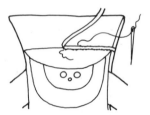

Pattern Pieces (see pages 114 through 115)

BODY (2), SLEEVE (2), SKIRT (2) from BODY fabric
HAT (2), APRON (2+1 Interfacing), WAISTBAND and TIE
    (3), LEG (2) from HAT fabric
FACE (1), HAND (2) from FACE fabric
SHOE (2), EYE (2) from SHOE fabric
HAIR FRONT (1), HAIR BUN (1) from HAIR fabric
CHEEK (2) from CHEEK fabric
MOUTH (1) from MOUTH fabric

Materials Required

BODY fabric, 9 by 12 inches of red cotton fabric with
    white pin-dots
HAT fabric, 9 by 12 inches of white batiste
FACE fabric, 2 by 3 inches of white felt
SHOE fabric, 3 by 5 inches of black felt
HAIR fabric, 3 by 4 inches of brown felt
CHEEK fabric, bright pink felt scrap
MOUTH fabric, red felt scrap
Apron and Pantalette trim, ⅓ yard of ½-inch-wide
    lace edging
Hat trim, ¾ yard of ⅛-inch-wide pale blue satin rib-
    bon
Stuffing, polyester fiber filling

Making the Doll

Cut out all pieces.

The Miniature
Sea Captain's Wife

Captain Simon's wife, Edith, is a hard-working woman.
She is made of red with white pin-dot cotton. Her
apron and pantalettes are white batiste trimmed with
cobwebby white lace. She has brown felt hair and a
pale blue satin ribbon trims her hat.

STEP 1. MAKING THE BODY FRONT AND BACK

A. Baste FACE to the right side of one BODY section
at the dotted line position, as shown on pattern, and
stitch close to the outer edges.

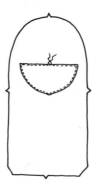

B. Baste HAIR FRONT to the right side of body front, matching the notches and with the raw edges even.

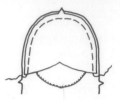

C. Pin HAIR BUN to the right side of remaining BODY section at the solid line position. Stitch across top of bun by hand, as shown in the drawing.

STEP 2. MAKING THE SLEEVES, SHOES, AND LEGS

A. Baste a HAND to the right side of each SLEEVE, matching the notches.

B. Fold each sleeve in half, with right sides facing. Stitch, leaving the slanted edge open. Turn the sleeve right side out, baste the raw edges together, and press. Baste the sleeves to the right side of body front, matching the notches.

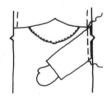

C. Fold each SHOE, as shown in the drawing, and stitch from A to B. Turn each shoe right side out. Fold extension over the shoes and stitch across fold, forming heel.

D. Stitch the long seam on each LEG. Turn right side out, bringing the seam to the center back. Turn under ¼ inch on lower edge of legs. Slip the extension of each shoe into the bottom of a leg and sew together by hand.

E. Sew trim by hand to lower edge of each leg, as shown in the drawing.

F. Baste two pleats at top of each leg, as shown. Baste legs to the right side of the lower edge of body front, with edges meeting at the center. Stitch legs in place.

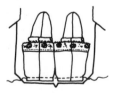

STEP 3. ASSEMBLING THE BODY

A. Baste the remaining BODY section to the body front, with right sides facing. Stitch, keeping the sleeves and legs tucked into the body and leaving an opening at bottom.

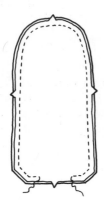

B. Turn body right side out. Stuff it firmly to within 1 inch of leg tops. Baste and then stitch 1 inch from leg tops to hold stuffing in place. Sew the bottom opening closed by hand.

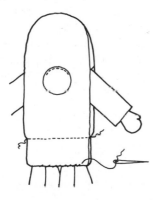

STEP 4. MAKING THE SKIRT AND APRON

A. Turn under ¼ inch on the lower edge of SKIRT and machine-stitch. Pin skirt sections together, with right sides facing. Stitch up the sides from the lower edge to the notches. Make two pleats at the upper edges of the front and back of skirt, following arrows on pattern, and baste. Turn under ¼ inch on upper and side edges and machine-stitch, stitching pleats in place.

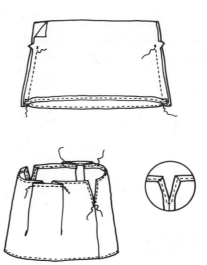

B. Place the skirt on the doll, matching the side seams and slipping arms through openings, and bring skirt to ⅛ inch under chin. Sew skirt securely to body by hand through all layers.

C. Pin APRON sections together, with right sides facing. Stitch along the sides and lower edge. Turn the apron right side out. Make two pleats at the upper edge, following arrows on pattern, and baste. Sew edging by hand to the lower edge of apron, as shown in the drawing.

45

D. Center and pin apron to apron WAISTBAND, with notches matching and with right sides together. Stitch and press seam allowances toward waistband. Turn in ¼ inch on remaining long edge and sew over seam allowances.

E. Pin apron to front over skirt, turning in ends of waistband at sides. Sew waistband in place at sides.

F. Turn in ¼ inch on all edges of TIES. Fold tie in half lengthwise, with wrong sides facing, and stitch close to the edges. Sew one end of ties to back at sides, and tie other ends together in a knot.

STEP 5. FINISHING THE DOLL

A. Glue EYES, CHEEKS, and MOUTH to the face, as shown in the drawing. If you prefer, you may embroider mouth with red embroidery cotton.

B. Pin HAT sections together, with right sides facing. Stitch, leaving an opening. Turn hat right side out, sew the opening closed by hand, and press. Run a gathering stitch ¼ inch from edges of the hat, as shown.

C. Place the hat on the doll, with the straight edge at the back. Pull up the gathers and adjust them evenly. Knot the gathering thread securely. Remove hat and sew gathers into place by machine. Cover gathering threads with ribbon. Secure ribbon in place with tiny stitches. Tie tiny bows and sew them into place at sides of hat, as shown.

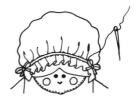

The Miniature Fisherman

Frederic the Fisherman is ready for a day of fishing. He is made of medium-weight slicker yellow cotton. His fasteners are black ½-inch dress hooks and his beard is chestnut brown felt.

Pattern Pieces (see pages 113 and 114)

BODY (2), SLEEVE (2), COAT (2), COLLAR (2), HAT FRONT (2), HAT BACK (2) of BODY fabric
BOOT (2), BOOT TOP (2), EYE (2) of BOOT fabric
FACE (1), HAND (2) of FACE fabric
BEARD (1) of BEARD fabric
NOSE (1) of NOSE fabric

Materials Required

BODY fabric, 9 by 27 inches of bright yellow medium-weight cotton
BOOT fabric, 9 by 4 inches of black felt
FACE fabric, 2 by 4 inches of white felt
BEARD fabric, 3 by 3 inches of chestnut brown felt
NOSE fabric, red felt scrap
Jacket trim, 4 hooks, ½ inch long
Stuffing, polyester fiber filling

Making the Doll

Cut out all pieces.

STEP 1. MAKING THE BODY FRONT

A. Baste the FACE to the right side of one BODY section at the dotted line position, as shown on pattern, and stitch close to the outer edges.

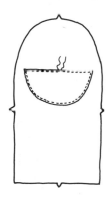

B. Glue BEARD to the face, with upper raw edges even, leaving bottom free.

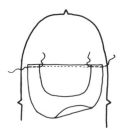

47

STEP 2. MAKING THE SLEEVES AND BOOTS

A. Baste a HAND to the right side of each SLEEVE, matching the notches.

B. Fold each sleeve in half, with right sides facing. Stitch, leaving the slanted edge open. Turn the sleeve right side out, baste the raw edges together, and press. Baste the sleeves to the right side of body front, matching the notches.

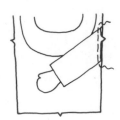

C. Fold each BOOT, as shown in the drawing, and stitch from A to B. Turn each boot right side out. Fold extension over boots and stitch across fold, forming heel.

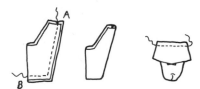

D. Stitch the long seam on each BOOT TOP. Turn right side out, bringing the seam to the center back. Slip the extension of the boots into the bottom of the boot tops and sew together by hand.

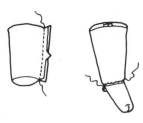

E. Baste boots to the right side of the lower edge of body front, with the edges overlapping at center, as shown. Stitch boots in place.

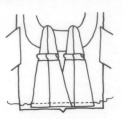

STEP 3. ASSEMBLING THE BODY

A. Baste the remaining BODY section to the body front, with right sides facing. Stitch, keeping the sleeves and boots tucked into the body and leaving an opening at bottom.

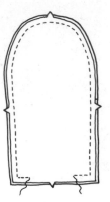

B. Turn body right side out. Stuff it firmly to within 1 inch of boot tops. Stitch 1 inch from boot tops to hold stuffing in place. Sew the bottom opening closed by hand.

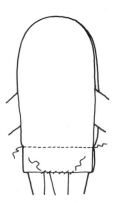

STEP 4. MAKING THE COLLAR AND JACKET

A. Pin COLLAR sections together, with right sides facing. Stitch, leaving an opening. Carefully clip to the inward corners, as shown. Turn right side out, press, and sew the opening closed by hand. Wrap collar around body with the points meeting just below the bottom of the beard. Sew the collar in place.

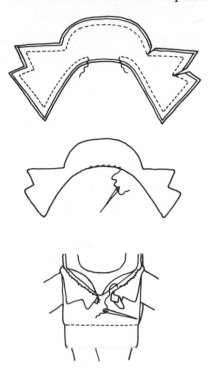

B. Pin COAT sections together, with right sides facing. Stitch, leaving an opening. Turn right side out, press, and sew the opening closed by hand.

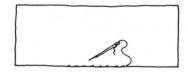

C. Wrap coat around body, overlapping at right side of doll, and sew in place. Sew four hooks to coat with prongs up, as shown in the drawing.

STEP 5. FINISHING THE DOLL

A. Stitch one HAT FRONT to one HAT BACK along the notched edge, with right sides facing. Stitch the other HAT FRONT to the other HAT BACK to make a lining. Stitch hat to hat lining with right sides facing and leaving an opening.

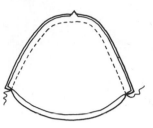

B. Turn right side out, press, and sew the opening closed. Place hat on doll, turning up front edge, and secure it in place at sides.

C. Glue EYES and NOSE to face, as shown in the drawing.

The Miniature Union and Confederate Soldiers

Ned and Harry have long since put down their rifles, but like to wear their uniforms just the same. Ned, the Confederate Soldier, is made of gray cotton canvas, and Harry, his Union counterpart, is navy blue canvas. Both gentlemen have black felt belts with tiny brass buckles, which are available at shoe-repair shops. Their hair and mustaches are chestnut brown felt, and Ned has a dashing goatee.

Pattern Pieces for Each (see page 113)

BODY (2), SLEEVE (2), JACKET (2), BRIM (2) from BODY fabric

BOOT (2), BOOT TOP (2), BELT (1), EYE (2) from BOOT fabric

FACE (1), HAND (2) from FACE fabric

SIDEBURN (2), MUSTACHE (1), GOATEE (1 for Ned only), HAIR BACK (1) from HAIR fabric

Materials Required for Each

BODY fabric, 9 by 16 inches of gray or navy blue cotton canvas

BOOT fabric, 9 by 5 inches of black felt

FACE fabric, 2 by 4 inches of white felt

HAIR fabric, 3 by 4 inches of chestnut brown felt
Jacket and Hat trim, 1/3 yard of ⅛-inch-wide gold braid
Jacket buttons, six ¼-inch brass ball buttons
Stuffing, polyester fiber filling

Making the Dolls

Cut out all pieces.

STEP 1. MAKING THE BODY FRONT

A. Baste FACE to the right side of one BODY section at the dotted line position, as shown on pattern, and stitch close to the outer edges.

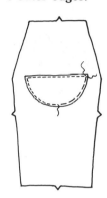

B. By hand, stitch SIDEBURNS to face, as shown in the drawing, using tiny stitches.

STEP 2. MAKING THE SLEEVES AND BOOTS

A. Sew gold braid by hand to each SLEEVE, forming a point, as shown in the drawing. Baste a HAND to the right side of each sleeve, matching the notches.

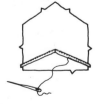

B. Fold each sleeve in half, with right sides facing. Stitch, leaving the slanted edge open. Turn each sleeve right side out, baste the raw edges together, and press. Baste the sleeves to the right side of body front, matching the notches.

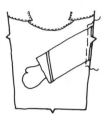

C. Fold each BOOT, as shown in the drawing, and stitch from A to B. Turn each boot right side out. Fold extension over boots and stitch across fold, forming heel.

D. Stitch the long seam on each BOOT TOP. Turn right side out, bringing the seam to the center back. Slip the extension of the boots into the bottom of the boot tops, and sew together by hand.

E. Baste boots to the right side of the lower edge of body front, with the edges overlapping at center, as shown. Stitch boots in place.

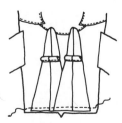

STEP 3. ASSEMBLING THE BODY

A. By hand, stitch HAIR BACK to the right side of remaining BODY section at dotted line position, using tiny stitches.

B. Baste the remaining body section to body front, with right sides facing. Stitch, keeping the sleeves and boots tucked into the body and leaving an opening at the bottom.

C. Turn body right side out. Stuff body firmly to within 1 inch from boot tops. Stitch 1 inch from boot tops to hold stuffing in place. Sew the bottom opening closed by hand. Squeeze top of body together and sew pleat together for hat, as shown in the drawing.

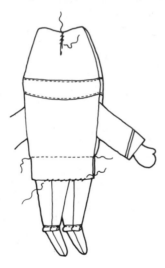

STEP 4. MAKING THE JACKET AND HAT

A. Pin JACKET sections together, with right sides facing. Stitch, leaving one long edge open. Turn jacket right side out, press, and baste the raw edges together.

B. Encase basted edges of jacket with BELT. Stitch close to the edges of belt, and fasten a buckle to the straight end.

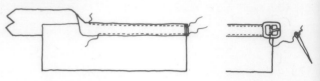

C. Wrap jacket around body under sleeves. Buckle the belt and sew in place by hand.

D. Stitch ends of each BRIM and press seam open. Pin both brim sections together, with right sides facing, and stitch the outer edges together. Trim. Turn right side out and press. Turn under ¼ inch on inner curved edges and stitch together. Sew gold braid over the inner curved edge.

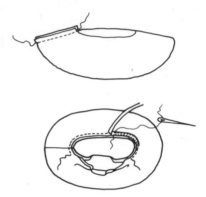

E. Place brim over body. Sew brim in place along the brim seam. Turn up the right side of brim and tack to body, as shown.

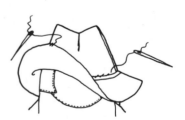

STEP 5. FINISHING THE DOLL

A. Glue EYES and MUSTACHE to face. For Ned glue GOATEE to face.

B. Sew six gold buttons to body front.

The Miniature Southern Belle

Marilyn is a delicate belle from an Old Southern plantation. She is made of a pink and white cotton, and her pink felt hat and shoes match her velvet ribbon trim. The tiny flower nosegay she holds is trimmed with the delicate lace that also trims her skirt and pantalettes.

Pattern Pieces (see page 114)

BODY (2), SLEEVE (2), SKIRT (2), SKIRT RUFFLE (3) cut a rectangular pattern 1½ by 12 inches, SLEEVE RUF-FLE (2) cut a rectangular pattern 1½ by 3¾ inches, NOSEGAY HOLDER (1) of BODY fabric
LEG (2) from LEG fabric
HAT FRONT (1), HAT BACK (1), BRIM (1), SHOE (2) from HAT fabric
FACE (1), HAND (2) from FACE fabric
HAIR FRONT (1), HAIR BACK (1), CURL (3) from HAIR fabric
EYE (2), from EYE fabric
CHEEK (2) from CHEEK fabric
MOUTH (1) from MOUTH fabric

Materials Required

BODY fabric, 9 by 21 inches of bright pink and white cotton
LEG fabric, 2 by 7 inches of white batiste
HAT fabric, 5 by 9 inches of bright pink felt
FACE fabric, 2 by 3 inches of white felt
HAIR fabric, 9 by 3 inches of chestnut brown felt
EYE fabric, black felt scrap
CHEEK fabric, bright pink felt scrap
MOUTH fabric, red felt scrap
NOSEGAY, tiny artificial flowers
Dress and Nosegay trim, 1 yard of 1-inch-wide lace and ⅔ yard of ¼ inch wide bright pink ribbon
Stuffing, polyester fiber filling

Making the Doll

Cut out all pieces.

STEP 1. MAKING THE BODY FRONT AND BACK

A. Baste the FACE to the right side of one BODY section at the dotted line position, as shown on pattern, and stitch close to the outer edges.

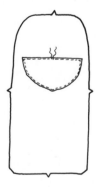

B. Baste HAIR FRONT to the right side of body front, matching the notches and with the raw edges even. Baste HAT FRONT to the right side of hair front, matching the notches and with the raw edges even.

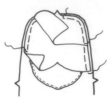

C. Baste HAIR BACK to the right side of the remaining BODY section, matching the notches and with the raw edges even. Baste HAT BACK to the right side of hair back, matching the notches and with the raw edges even.

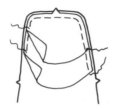

STEP 2. MAKING THE SLEEVES AND SHOES

A. Baste each HAND to the right side of a SLEEVE, matching the notches.

B. Fold each sleeve in half, with right sides facing. Stitch, leaving the slanted edge open. Turn the sleeve right side out, baste the raw edges together, and press.

C. For SLEEVE RUFFLES, use two rectangles, each 1½ inches long and 3¾ inches wide. Turn under ¼ inch

on long edges and machine-stitch. Fold the ruffle, with right sides facing, and stitch the short side. Turn right side out. Run a gathering stitch ¼ inch from upper edge. Place the ruffle on the sleeve, with lower edge of ruffle covering bottom edge of sleeve. Pull up the gathers and adjust them evenly. Knot the gathering threads securely and sew the ruffle in place by machine.

D. Baste the sleeves to the right side of body front, matching the notches.

E. Fold each SHOE, as shown in the drawing, and stitch from A to B. Turn each shoe right side out. Fold extension over shoes and stitch across each fold, forming heels.

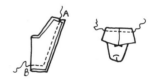

F. Stitch the notched seam on each LEG. Turn right side out, bringing the seam to the center. Turn under ¼ inch on lower edge of each leg. Slip the extension of each shoe into the bottom of each leg and sew together by hand. Sew two layers of lace trim to each leg, as shown in the drawing. Baste two pleats at top of each leg, as shown.

G. Baste legs to the right side of the lower edge of body front, with edges meeting at center. Stitch legs in place.

STEP 3. ASSEMBLING THE BODY

A. Baste the remaining body section to the body front, with right sides facing. Stitch, keeping the sleeves and legs tucked into the body and leaving an opening at bottom.

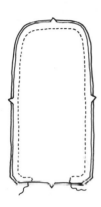

B. Turn body right side out. Stuff it firmly to within 1 inch of leg tops. Stitch 1 inch from leg tops to hold stuffing in place. Sew the opening closed.

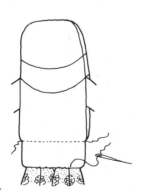

STEP 4. MAKING THE SKIRT

A. Turn under ¼ inch on upper and lower edges of SKIRT and machine-stitch. Pin skirt sections together, with right sides facing, and stitch the sides. Turn right side out.

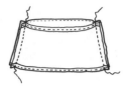

B. For SKIRT RUFFLES, use three rectangles, each 1½ inches long and 12 inches wide. Turn under ¼ inch on long edges and machine-stitch. Fold the ruffle, with right sides facing, and stitch the short side. Turn right side out. Run a gathering stitch ¼ inch from upper edge.

C. Starting at the bottom, pin the ruffles to the skirt, at the lower edge, at the center, and along the top edge, with right sides up and seams at one side. Pull up gathers and adjust them evenly. Knot the gathering thread securely. Stitch ruffles into place by machine.

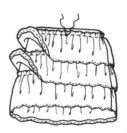

D. Place the skirt on the doll and sew it securely in place. Cover the gathering threads on the upper ruffle with ribbon and sew in place. Sew lace trim underneath lower ruffle, as shown in the drawing.

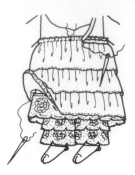

STEP 5. FINISHING THE DOLL

A. Glue EYES, CHEEKS, and MOUTH to the face, as shown in the drawing. If you prefer, you may embroider mouth with red embroidery cotton.

B. Place BRIM over the hat, with the raw edges even at front. Lift up the front brim and sew it in place between body seams, by hand. Turn down the front brim. Tie a piece of ribbon into bow and sew it to back brim.

C. Starting at the bottom, wrap CURL into a curl and sew the ends securely in place. Sew curls to right side of head, as shown in the drawing.

D. Turn under ¼ inch on the curved edge of NOSE-GAY HOLDER and machine-stitch. Fold nosegay holder, with right sides facing, and stitch the straight edge. Turn right side out. Sew a gathered piece of lace to the open end of nosegay.

E. Insert tiny artificial flowers inside nosegay and sew them in place. Tie a ribbon into a bow and sew to nosegay, as shown in the drawing. Sew nosegay securely to right hand of doll.

CHAPTER 5

Seven Stuffed Animals

Here is a group of seven stylized stuffed animals with two distinctive constructions. The five wool and velveteen animals—Tedda Bear and Four Friends—have a unique round and chubby arm and leg construction. Their height is approximately 9 inches. Faces are made of three pieces, two sides and one triangular snout piece, so that each has a realistically shaped head. The Lion and Tiger, on the other hand, are made of cotton and have flat, pillow-shaped heads and flat legs. They are larger than the other animals, about 13 inches in height. Both sets of animals have button eyes and are trimmed with bows. The Lion and Tiger have felt features and the other five have embroidered ones.

Tedda Bear
and Four Friends

While most bears are called "Teddy," my bear is a "Tedda" bear, named after a most special friend. Tedda Bear and his companions—Rusty Rabbit, Barry Panda, Nicholas Pig, and Florrie Kitten— are all cut using the same pattern pieces for the body, legs, and head. Their ears and tails are different, and the pig has a cleft in his hooves. The wrap-around construction of the upper and lower legs makes these animals distinctive among stuffed toys.

Four of the animals are constructed of wool coating fabric, which has a stretchy quality; when the animals are stuffed, they are quite plump. Because pigs are not as furry as the other animals, I used velveteen to construct Nicholas, and, since velveteen does not stretch like coating fabric, I used only ⅛-inch seams on his head and body. As a result, when stuffed, the pig is as plump as the other animals.

These animals could be made of wool coating, wool flannel, velveteen, corduroy, lightweight fake fur, or plush. The linings for the rabbit and kitten ears could be made of felt, velveteen, or lightweight cotton. All the animals are dressed in their finest vests and bow ties to go out and meet the world. Their vests are made of solid color cotton velveteens, but any wool, cotton, corduroy, or velvet in solids, plaids, stripes, or prints would be effective. I like to make the collars of white cotton duck or drill. The ribbon bow ties could be grosgrain, velvet, moire, or satin, as well as the gingham that I have used.

Pattern Pieces for Bear and Friends (see pages 116 through 118)

HEAD SIDE (2), SNOUT (1), BODY FRONT (1), HEAD and BODY BACK (1), BOTTOM and SIDE (1), UPPER LEG (2), LOWER LEG (2), UPPER PAW (2), LOWER PAW (2) from BODY fabric (* for Panda see below)
VEST FRONT (4), VEST BACK (2) from VEST fabric
COLLAR (2) from COLLAR fabric

Extra Pattern Pieces for Bear

BEAR EAR (4) of BODY fabric

Extra Pattern Pieces for Rabbit

RABBIT EAR BACK (2), RABBIT TAIL (2) from BODY fabric
RABBIT EAR FRONT (2) from RABBIT EAR FRONT fabric

Extra Pattern Pieces for Panda Bear

PANDA EAR (4), EYE PATCH (2) from LEG fabric (*Legs and paws are also cut of LEG fabric instead of BODY fabric, as in "Tedda" Bear.)

Extra Pattern Pieces for Pig

PIG EAR (4), PIG NOSE (2), PIG TAIL (1) from BODY fabric (Be sure to cut PIG UPPER LEG, LOWER LEG, UPPER PAW, and LOWER PAW following Pig cutting lines.)

Extra Pattern Pieces for Kitten

KITTEN EAR (2), KITTEN TAIL (2) from BODY fabric
KITTEN EAR (2) from EAR LINING fabric

Materials Required for Bear

BODY fabric, ¼ yard of rust brown wool coating
VEST fabric, 9 by 16 inches of hunter green velveteen
COLLAR fabric, 9 by 10 inches of white cotton duck
EYES, two ⅝-inch black buttons
NOSE and MOUTH, black six-strand embroidery thread
Bow tie, ½ yard of 1½-inch-wide royal blue and white gingham ribbon
Vest trim, three ⅜-inch white shirt buttons
Stuffing, polyester fiber filling

Materials Required for Rabbit

BODY fabric, ¼ yard of white wool coating
RABBIT EAR FRONT fabric, 4 by 6 inches of bright pink velveteen or felt
VEST fabric, 9 by 16 inches of orange velveteen
COLLAR fabric, 9 by 10 inches of white cotton duck
EYES, two ½-inch red buttons
NOSE and MOUTH, pink six-strand embroidery thread
Bow tie, ½ yard of 1½-inch-wide pink and white gingham ribbon
Vest trim, three ⅜-inch white shirt buttons
Ear wires, 2 long pipe cleaners
Stuffing, polyester fiber filling

Materials Required for Panda

BODY fabric, 9 by 20 inches of white wool coating
LEG fabric, 9 by 20 inches of black wool coating
VEST fabric, 9 by 16 inches of red velveteen
COLLAR fabric, 9 by 10 inches of white cotton duck
EYES, two ⅝-inch white buttons
NOSE, black six-strand embroidery thread
MOUTH, red six-strand embroidery thread
Bow tie, ½ yard of 1½-inch-wide yellow and white gingham ribbon
Vest trim, three ⅜-inch white buttons
Stuffing, polyester fiber filling

Materials Required for Pig

BODY fabric, ¼ yard of bright pink velveteen
VEST fabric, 9 by 16 inches of yellow velveteen
COLLAR fabric, 9 by 10 inches of white cotton duck
EYES, two ½-inch red buttons
Bow tie, ½ yard of 1½-inch-wide emerald green and white gingham ribbon
Vest trim, three ⅜-inch white shirt buttons
Stuffing, polyester fiber filling

Materials Required for Kitten

BODY fabric, ¼ yard of white wool coating
EAR LINING fabric, 4 by 6 inches of pale pink felt or velveteen
VEST fabric, 9 by 16 inches of bright pink velveteen
COLLAR fabric, 9 by 10 inches of white cotton duck
EYES, two ½-inch French-blue buttons
NOSE, pale pink six-strand embroidery thread
MOUTH, bright pink six-strand embroidery thread
WHISKERS, four 6-inch lengths of white raffia, ⅛-inch white ribbon, waxed heavy white cotton thread, or fishing line
Bow tie, ½ yard of 1½-inch-wide French-blue and white gingham ribbon
Vest trim, three ⅜-inch white shirt buttons
Stuffing, polyester fiber filling

Making the Dolls

Cut out all pieces except for bows.

STEP 1. MAKING THE HEAD AND BODY

A. With right sides facing, stitch the center seam of each HEAD SIDE from A to B. Press seam open.

B. Baste the SNOUT to upper edge of the head side, right sides facing, matching points A and notches. Stitch, then carefully clip the curves. Press seams open.

C. With right sides facing, pin the head front to BODY FRONT. Match the notches and stitch the neck seam, then press the seam open.

D. Pin the head and body front to HEAD and BODY BACK, with right sides facing. Stitch the head seam only, ending stitching at the neck.

E. Pin BOTTOM and SIDE to the body front and back, right sides facing, matching the notches. First, stitch the front seam, starting at one neck edge and ending at the other; then stitch the back seam, starting at the neck edge, leaving an opening at the bottom, and finishing to the other neck edge.

F. Turn the whole piece right side out and stuff it firmly. Turn in the opening edges and sew them closed.

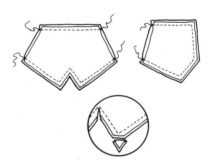

STEP 2. MAKING THE VEST AND COLLAR

A. Pin VEST FRONT and VEST BACK to their corresponding lining pieces, with right sides facing. Stitch all edges, leaving the side seams open. Trim the corners, clip the inward corners on vest back, and turn the pieces right side out. Press.

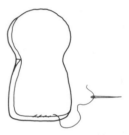

B. With right sides up, overlap LEFT VEST FRONT over RIGHT VEST FRONT about ¼ inch. With right sides facing, pin vest front to vest back at side seams. Try the vest on the body, wrong sides out, and adjust the fit if necessary. Unpin front edges. Stitch the side seams, and press them open.

C. Place the vest on the body, right side out, and overlap the front edges as before. Pin in place. Sew three ⅜-inch buttons to vest front through all layers.

D. (Note: Before sewing the collar, test fit with paper pattern. The unsewn collar should overlap about ⅛ inch at front top.) Pin COLLAR sections together, with right sides facing. Stitch all edges, leaving an opening. Trim the corners, carefully clip the inward curve, then turn the collar right side out. Turn in the opening edges and sew them closed. Press.

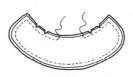

E. Place collar over the vest and tack in place at the front upper edge.

STEP 3. MAKING THE LEGS

A. With right sides facing, fold each UPPER LEG and LOWER LEG, matching the notches. Stitch between A and B on each.

B. With right sides facing and matching the notches, baste a PAW to each corresponding leg, and stitch. (For pig legs only clip to inward corners.)

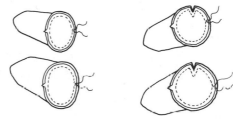

Pig

C. Turn legs right side out. Turn in ¼ inch on opening edges and baste. Stuff legs firmly, leaving some room at the basted edges.

D. First, pin the lower legs to the body, having legs curve around body, back edge even with the back seams. Then pin the upper legs to the body above the lower legs, as shown in the drawing.

E. Check to see if the body balances on the lower legs. Adjust the leg positions if necessary. Sew legs securely to body along the basted edges. Tack the front of the legs to the body.

STEP 4. MAKING THE EARS

A. For bear or panda, stitch dart in BEAR EAR (or PANDA EAR) and trim. Stitch the ear sections together with right sides facing, leaving an opening. Turn ears right side out and sew opening closed.

B. For rabbit or pig, stitch RABBIT EAR FRONT and RABBIT EAR BACK (or PIG EAR) sections together, with right sides facing and leaving the straight edge open. Trim the corner, turn the ears right side out, and press. Cut a pipe cleaner for each ear, measuring twice the length of ear. Fold the pipe cleaners in half, insert them into the ears, and sew the opening closed. For the rabbit, make a small pleat at the bottom of each ear and tack in place.

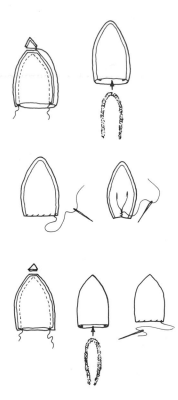

C. For kitten, stitch KITTEN EAR sections together, with right sides facing and leaving an opening. Trim corners, turn ears right side out, and sew opening

closed. Press. Fold the ear over the contrast side at the line indicated and tack in place.

D. For all the animals, pin ears to the corresponding head at the desirable position (with lining side facing front on rabbit and kitten). Sew them securely in place. Bend pig ears forward.

Kitten   Bear and Panda

Rabbit   Pig

STEP 5. MAKING THE TAILS

A. For pig, turn in ¼ inch on all edges of PIG TAIL and baste. Fold the tail lengthwise, with the wrong sides facing, and sew the basted edges together, leaving the short end open. Insert a pipe cleaner into the tail and sew the opening closed. Wrap the tail around your finger to form a curl.

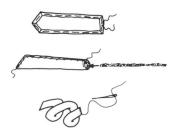

B. For rabbit, stitch RABBIT TAIL sections together, with right sides facing, leaving an opening. Turn the tail right side out, stuff it lightly, and sew the opening closed.

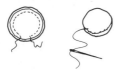

C. For kitten, stitch KITTEN TAIL sections together, with the right sides facing, leaving an opening. Carefully clip the inward curve, trim the corners, and turn the tail right side out. Stuff the tail firmly and sew the opening closed.

D. For all the animals, pin tails to corresponding bottom back and sew them securely in place. The bears do not have tails.

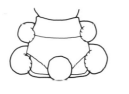

Rabbit

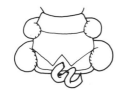

Pig

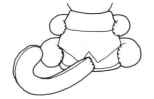

Kitten

STEP 6. MAKING THE EYES

A. For bear, sew two ⅝-inch black buttons to the face, as shown.

B. For panda, turn in ¼ inch on all edges of each EYE PATCH and pin them to the face. Sew them in place, then sew two ⅝-inch white buttons to the patches, as shown.

C. For pig and rabbit, sew two ½-inch red buttons to the face, as shown.

D. For kitten, sew two ½-inch light blue buttons to the face, as shown.

STEP 7. MAKING THE NOSES

A. For bear and panda, using six strands of black embroidery floss, embroider the nose in a satin stitch, as shown.

B. For pig, stitch NOSE sections together, with the right sides facing and leaving an opening. Turn the nose right side out, sew the opening closed, and sew to face, as shown.

C. For rabbit, using six strands of pink embroidery floss, embroider the nose in a straight stitch, as shown.

D. For kitten, using pale pink embroidery floss, embroider the nose in a satin stitch, as shown.

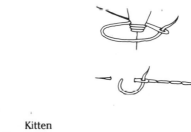

Kitten

Panda

Rabbit

Pig

Bear

63

STEP 8. MAKING THE MOUTHS

A. For bear, using six strands of black embroidery floss, embroider the mouth in a straight stitch, as shown.

B. For panda, using six strands of red embroidery floss, embroider the mouth in a straight stitch, as shown.

C. For rabbit, using six strands of pink embroidery floss, embroider the mouth in a straight stitch, as shown.

D. For kitten, using six strands of bright pink embroidery floss, embroider the mouth in a straight stitch and sew whiskers to each side of the snout, using raffia, ⅛-inch ribbon, or fishing line.

STEP 9. MAKING THE BOW TIE

A. Use ½ yard of 1½-inch wide gingham ribbon. Cut 1½ inches off and save this small piece for the knot. Fold the larger piece of ribbon to make a double bow, as shown, with the raw ends hidden inside the bow. Tack the center of the bow securely.

B. Fold both raw ends of small piece to back to form a piece ¾ inch wide. Wrap this around the center of the bow tie, and sew the edges together at the back of the bow.

C. Sew the bow tie in place at the center of the collar.

C-1. The Three American Couples are all made with the same easy technique. Present are Daniel and Mrs. Boone (top); the Southern Colonel and Belle (center), and the New England Sea Captain and his wife. See Chapter 2.

C-2. Gathered around the table are miniature versions (5 to 6 inches) of some American figures. From right to left are Confederate and Union soldiers, a fisherman, a Southern belle, and a sea captain and his wife. See Chapter 4.

C-3. The brother, sister, and baby girl of this rag doll family are easy to make and their clothes are detachable and washable. See Chapter 6.

C-4. Three accessories for a child's room are the Gingham Pajama-Bag Doll (center), the Flying Angel Pillow-Doll (right), and the Cupid Pillow-Doll (left). See Chapter 7.

C-5. Except for facial features, Tedda Bear and his four friends are basically the same doll. Instructions are in Chapter 5.

C-6. Louis the Lion Tamer is one of the Three Working Men featured in Chapter 3. He is shown here with Leon the Lion and Maurice the Tiger from Chapter 5.

C-7. Pictured are three accessories for a child's room. The Policeman (left) and the Engineer (center) are made the same way as Louis the Lion Tamer from Chapter 3. The French Sailor Pillow-Doll is just right for a boy's bed. In the foreground are Virginia and Vicente, two pot-holder dolls for the kitchen. See Chapter 7.

C-1

The Lion and the Tiger

Both Leon the Lion and Maurice the Tiger are of the same basic easy construction. Except for the heads, the ears, and the noses, and, of course, the lion's wonderful mane, which is made of thirty-five tiny cotton bows, the pattern pieces for the lion and tiger are identical. Maurice and Leon were trained by Louis the Lion Tamer (see page 36) and the three make an entertaining grouping for a child's room.

Pattern Pieces for Lion and Tiger (see pages 119 through 120)

BODY (2), BODY SIDE (2), BOTTOM (1), PAW (4), TAIL (2), from BODY fabric
CHEEK (2) from CHEEK fabric
MOUTH (1) from MOUTH fabric

Extra Pattern Pieces for Lion

EAR (4) from BODY fabric
MANE (35) and TAIL TRIM (2) cut a rectangular pattern, 2 by 6½ inches, from MANE fabric
NOSE (1) from NOSE fabric
NOSE TRIANGLE (1) from NOSE TRIANGLE fabric

Extra Pattern Pieces for Tiger

EAR (4) from EAR fabric
NOSE (1) from NOSE fabric
NOSE TRIANGLE (1) from NOSE TRIANGLE fabric

Materials Required for Lion and Tiger

BODY fabric, ½ yard marigold yellow cotton (with white stripes for Tiger)
CHEEK fabric, bright pink felt scrap
MOUTH fabric, magenta felt scrap
NOSE fabric, orange felt scrap
NOSE TRIANGLE fabric, red felt scrap
EYES, two ⅝-inch black buttons
WHISKERS, six 8-inch lengths of white raffia, fishing tackle, waxed cotton thread, or ⅛-inch-wide satin ribbon
Bow, 1 yard of 1½-inch-wide red with white polka-dot grosgrain ribbon
Claws, orange six-strand embroidery thread
Stuffing, polyester fiber filling

Additional Materials for Lion

MANE fabric, ⅜ yard of marigold yellow cotton with white pin-dots or stripes

Additional Materials for Tiger

EAR fabric, 9 by 6 inches of marigold yellow cotton

Making the Dolls

Cut out all pieces.

STEP 1. MAKING THE TIGER'S EARS

A. (For Lion, leave ears for later.) Stitch dart in TIGER EAR and trim. Stitch the ear sections together, with right sides facing, leaving the lower edge open. Turn ears right side out and baste raw edges together. Press.

B. Baste ears to right side of one BODY section, matching darts to the notches.

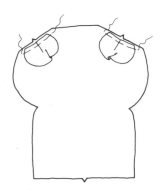

STEP 2. MAKING THE TAIL

A. Pin TAIL sections together, with right sides facing. Stitch, leaving the short, straight edge open.

B. Turn the tail right side out and stuff. Baste raw edges together. Baste tail to the right side of either short end of BOTTOM, matching notches.

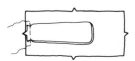

STEP 3. ASSEMBLING THE BODY

A. Pin body front to remaining BODY section, with right sides facing. Stitch head seam only, ending at the neck.

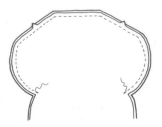

B. Stitch BODY SIDE sections to short ends of bottom, with right sides facing and notches matching..

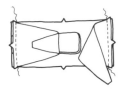

C. Pin bottom and sides to body front and back, with right sides facing and notches matching. First, stitch the front seam ending at the neck edge; then, stitch the back seam, starting at the neck edge and leaving an opening at the bottom.

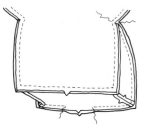

D. Turn the body right side out, stuff it firmly, and sew the opening closed.

STEP 4. MAKING THE LEGS

A. Pin LEG sections together, with right sides facing. Stitch, leaving an opening at the top.

B. Turn each leg right side out, stuff it firmly, and sew the opening closed. Using six strands of embroidery cotton, work three claws in a straight stitch at bottom on each leg, each stitch ⅝ inch long.

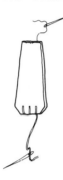

C. Pin the legs to the body front at neck edge, leaving a ½-inch space between the legs. Sew legs securely in place at upper edge.

STEP 5. MAKING THE FACE

A. Glue NOSE, NOSE TRIANGLE, MOUTH, and CHEEKS to the face. The top of the nose meets the top of the head.

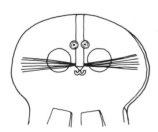

B. For eyes, sew two ⅝-inch black buttons on each side of upper edge of nose.

C. Sew whiskers to each side of nose.

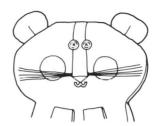

STEP 6. MAKING THE LION'S MANE AND EARS

A. Turn under ¼ inch on long edges of MANE pieces and machine-stitch. Fold in half, with right sides facing, forming bows, and stitch the short ends together. Turn bow right side out, bring seam to the center, and gather and wrap thread around bow. Complete thirty-five bows for mane and two bows for tail.

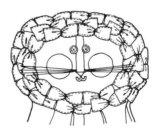

B. Start pinning bows to head front around face, leaving an oval 7 inches wide and 4 inches long. Then pin bows to head front and back along the outer seam, as shown. Fill in any empty spaces between the face and outer edge. Sew bows securely in place.

C. Pin LION EAR sections together, with right sides facing. Stitch, leaving an opening. Trim corners. Turn ears right side out, press, and sew the opening closed.

D. Make a small pleat at the bottom of each ear and tack in place. Sew ears to face at lower edge of top of mane, as shown in the drawing.

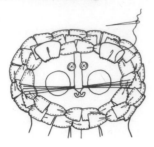

E. Cross two bows and sew to end of tail.

STEP 7. MAKING THE BOW TIE

A. Use 1 yard of 1½-inch-wide polka-dot ribbon for each animal. Cut a piece of ribbon 20 inches long. Fold the ribbon in half and stitch 4 inches and 9½ inches from fold.

B. Open out ribbon, forming a double bow, as shown. Fold a piece of 3½-inch-long ribbon in half. Stitch short ends together and turn right side out. This becomes the knot. Pull the double bow piece and the 12-inch piece of ribbon ends through ribbon knot. Bring ribbon ends down and secure to back of bow. Trim ends as shown.

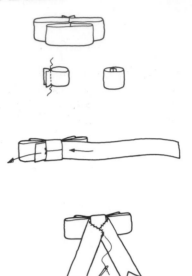

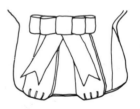

C. Sew bow to front neck, covering top of legs.

CHAPTER 6

A Rag Doll Family

My doll family consists of a brother, a sister, and a baby girl. They range in height from 18 to 20 inches. Their bodies are made of unbleached muslin, but they could also be made of cotton in a flesh tone. The most distinctive feature about these dolls is that their hair is made from fabric. Since I wanted each one to be a redhead, I used a bright orange cotton for the hair, but you can make them blondes or brunettes, if you prefer. The hair front and back pieces are sewn to the dolls and then covered with "yo-yo's" or pinked bow ties. The "yo-yo's," reminiscent of the gathered circles used to make turn-of-the-century quilts and coverlets, are fun to make.

The Boy and the Girl Dolls

The boy doll is named Wade after my own son, who is also a redhead. This Wade is dressed in short pants of pale blue felt and an ivory eyelet shirt. You might prefer to make his pants of velveteen or a lightweight wool flannel and his shirt of a lightweight cotton or linen.

The girl doll is named Brenda Sue. She wears a play dress and bloomers of ivory cotton eyelet. The pockets of her dress and her hair bow are made of matching eyelet border. The dress could be made of gingham or a light-hearted cotton print.

Pattern Pieces for Boy or Girl (see pages 121 through 129)

BODY FRONT (1), BODY BACK (1), ARM (4), LEG (2),
    FOOT (4), SOLE (2) from BODY fabric
HAIR FRONT (1), HAIR BACK (1), YO-YO (35 for boy, 36
    for girl) from HAIR fabric
EYE (2) from EYE fabric
CHEEK (2) from CHEEK fabric

Materials Required for Boy or Girl

BODY fabric, ⅜ yard of unbleached muslin
HAIR fabric, 1 yard of orange cotton
EYE, black felt scrap
CHEEK, bright pink felt scrap
MOUTH, bright pink six-strand embroidery thread

Making the Dolls

Cut out all pieces.

STEP 1. MAKING THE BODY FRONT

A. Use three strands of six-strand embroidery cotton in needle to work the MOUTH. Work mouth on BODY FRONT, in pink, with a satin stitch, as shown.

B. Baste HAIR FRONT to the body front, with right sides facing, matching center notches. Baste or pin and stitch at the center notch and sew each side to neck from this center point so hair will be centered on face. Carefully clip the hair front seam allowances, and press seam allowances toward hair front.

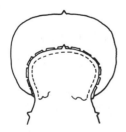

STEP 2. MAKING THE ARMS AND LEGS

A. Pin ARM sections together, with right sides facing. Stitch, leaving the straight edge open. Carefully clip to the inward corner and turn the arm right side out. Stuff the arm firmly and baste the opening closed.

B. Baste arms to the right side of the body front, with thumbs down, matching the notches.

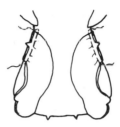

C. Stitch front and back seams of each FOOT, with the right sides facing. Stitch SOLE to each foot, with right sides facing and with notches matching at the seams. Turn the foot right side out.

D. Stitch long seam in each LEG, with right sides facing.

E. Baste the legs to the feet, with right sides facing, matching back seams and the notches to the front seams; then stitch. Turn leg up to right side. Stuff feet and legs and baste the top opening closed.

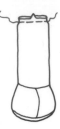

F. Make small tucks at sides of knees, as shown in the drawing, and stitch across knee through all layers.

G. Baste legs to the lower edge of body front, with front of leg facing right side; then machine-stitch.

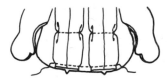

STEP 3. ASSEMBLING THE BODY

A. Stitch HAIR BACK to BODY BACK, with right sides facing and notches matching.

B. Baste the body back to the body front, with right sides facing. Stitch, keeping the arms and legs tucked into body and leaving the bottom open.

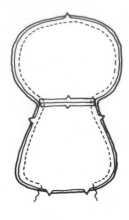

C. Carefully clip the inward curves and turn the body right side out. Stuff the body firmly and sew the opening closed.

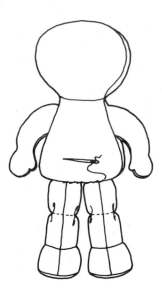

STEP 4. FINISHING THE HAIR AND FACE

A. Glue EYES and CHEEKS to the face, as shown.

B. Using a double strand of thread in needle, turn in ¼ inch on raw edges of YO-YO and hand-gather around the entire edge. Pull up the thread tightly and adjust the gathers. Knot the thread ends securely. Complete thirty-five yo-yo's for Wade and thirty-six yo-yo's for Brenda Sue. Pin yo-yo's to the doll's hair, distribute them evenly, and sew in place by hand.

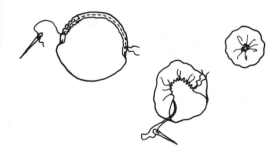

Pattern Pieces for Boy's Clothes (see pages 122 through 129)

SHORTS FRONT (2), SHORTS BACK (2), STRAP (4) from SHORTS fabric

SHORTS FRONT LINING (2), SHORTS BACK LINING (2) from SHORTS LINING fabric

SHIRT (2) from SHIRT fabric

SHOE (8), SOLE (4), T-STRAP (2), ANKLE STRAP (4) from SHOE fabric

Materials Required for Boy's Clothes

SHORTS fabric, ⅜ yard of pale blue felt, wool, or velveteen

SHORTS LINING fabric, 6 by 27 inches of pale blue lightweight cotton

SHIRT fabric, ¼ yard of ivory eyelet cotton

SHOE fabric, 9 by 36 inches of pale blue felt

Shirt trim, 1/3 yard of ¾- inch to 1-inch-wide ivory eyelet trim, 1 yard ⅛-inch-wide pale blue satin ribbon

Shoe trim, two ⅜-inch white buttons

Elastic, 1 yard of ¼-inch width

Pattern Pieces for Girl's Clothes (see pages 122 through 127)

DRESS (2) cut a rectangular pattern, 11 by 18 inches, PANTIES (2) cut a rectangular pattern, 6 by 12 inches, POCKET (2), BOW (1) cut a rectangular pattern, 3 by 22 inches of DRESS fabric, KNOT (1) cut a square pattern, 3 by 3 inches, of DRESS fabric

SHOE (8), SOLE (4), T-STRAP (2), ANKLE STRAP (4) from SHOE fabric

Materials Required for Girl's Clothes

DRESS fabric, ½ yard of ivory cotton eyelet or cotton print

SHOE fabric, 9 by 36 inches of pale pink felt

Dress trim, 1/3 yard of ¾- to 1-inch-wide ivory eyelet trim, 1 yard ⅛-inch-wide pale pink satin ribbon

Shoe trim, two ½-inch white buttons

Elastic, 1½ yards of ¼-inch width

Making the Clothes

Cut out all pieces.

STEP 1. MAKING THE GIRL'S DRESS

A. For dress, use two rectangles (one for front and one for back), each 11 inches long and 18 inches wide. Pin the front to the back, with right sides facing. Stitch the sides, leaving a 6-inch opening above stitching for the armholes. Turn under ¼ inch on armholes and machine-stitch.

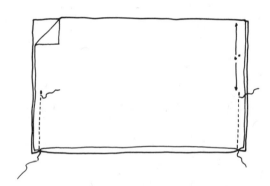

B. Turn up a 1-inch hem at bottom edge. Turn in ¼ inch on the raw edge and sew the hem in place.

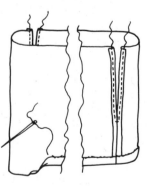

C. If you wish, place the upper edge of POCKET on the scalloped edge of your fabric, or, turn in ¼ inch on the straight edge and machine-stitch. In either case, turn in ¼ inch on the curved edge and baste. Place pockets on the front of the dress, as shown in the drawing, and stitch in place close to the curved outer edge of the pockets.

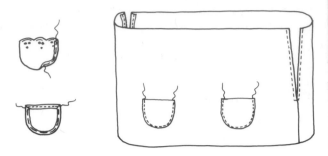

D. Turn down 2 inches at dress neck edge to form ruffle. Turn under ¼ inch on the raw edge and stitch in place. Stitch ⅜ inch above this stitching to form a casing. Run ¼-inch-wide (or narrower) elastic through the casing, place the dress on the doll, and draw up the elastic to form the neck ruffle. Secure the elastic ends together and tuck them inside dress.

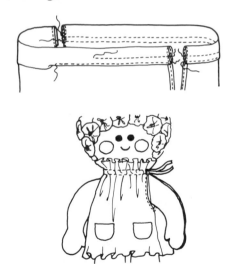

E. Pin ¾- to 1-inch-wide trim to the right side of the dress neck edge. Turn in one end at one side seam and sew in place by hand. Tie narrow ribbon into a bow and sew to front at neck.

F. For hair bow, use the 22- by 3-inch rectangle. Turn in ¼ inch on all edges. Turn in ¼ inch again and machine-stitch. Fold the fabric, forming a double bow, as shown in the drawing, with the ends hidden inside bow. Tack the center of the bow securely. For knot, cut a square 3 by 3 inches. Fold the raw ends back, wrap it around the center of the bow, and sew the edges together at the back of the bow, by hand. Sew the large bow to the head, by hand, as shown in the drawing.

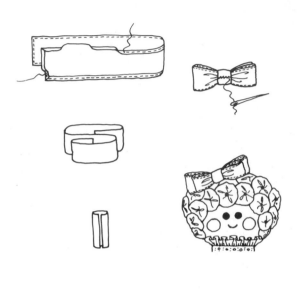

STEP 2. MAKING THE GIRL'S PANTIES

A. For panties, use two rectangles (one for front and one for back), each 6 inches long and 12 inches wide. Pin the back to the front and stitch the sides. Mark the center of the panties. Make a 1¾-inch slash at the center, as shown. Stitch around the slash, forming the crotch seam.

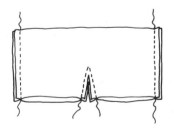

B. Turn down ⅝ inch at the upper edge to form waist casing. Turn in ¼ inch on the raw edge and stitch in place, leaving a small opening at one side. Turn up 1 inch at the lower edge, forming the leg casings. Turn in ¼ inch on the raw edge and stitch in place, leaving a small opening at sides. Stitch ⅜ below this stitching to form casing. Turn the panties right side out.

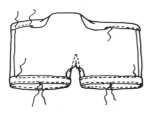

C. Run ¼-inch-wide (or narrower) elastic through casings, place the panties on the doll, and draw up the elastic. Secure the elastic ends together and sew the openings in the casing closed.

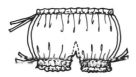

STEP 3. MAKING THE BOY'S SHIRT

A. Pin SHIRT sections together, with the right sides facing. Stitch the shoulder and underarm seams. Clip carefully to the inside corners and curves and turn the shirt right side out. Turn up ¼ inch on lower edge of shirt and machine-stitch.

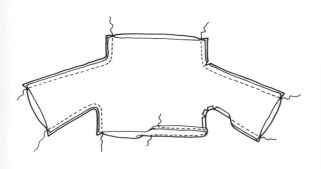

B. Turn in 1⅜ inches on neck and sleeves to form ruffles. Turn under ¼ inch on the raw edges and stitch in place, leaving a small opening. Stitch ⅜ inch away from this stitching to form casings. Run ¼-inch-wide (or narrower) elastic through the casings, place the shirt on the doll, and draw up the elastic. Secure the elastic ends together and sew the openings in the casing closed. Pin ¾- to 1-inch-wide trim to the right side of the shirt neck edge. Turn in one end at one side seam and sew in place by hand. Tie narrow ribbon into a bow and sew to front at neck.

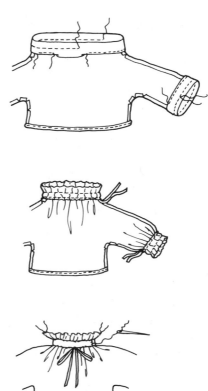

STEP 4. MAKING THE BOY'S SHORTS

A. Stitch the center front seam in SHORTS FRONT to the circle indicated on the pattern, with the right sides facing. Stitch the center back seam in SHORTS BACK, with right sides facing. Clip curves and clip to the front circle.

B. Stitch the shorts front to the shorts back at the side and inside leg edges. Turn the shorts right side out. Turn up ¼ inch on the leg openings and baste.

C. Prepare lining following Steps A and B, but do not turn to right side. Pin the lining to the shorts, with right sides facing. Stitch the waist and front opening edge to the circle. Trim the corners, turn the lining inside the shorts, and press. Sew the basted edges of the lining to shorts.

D. Sew two small snaps to the front opening, and place the shorts on the doll. Pin STRAP sections together, with right sides facing, and stitch the long edges. Turn the straps right side out, and press. Pin the straight ends of the straps to the front waist. Bring them around to the back, cross them, and pin to the back waist. Sew straps securely to shorts lining, with unfinished ends inside shorts.

STEP 5. MAKING THE SHOES

A. Pin SHOE sections together and stitch the front and back seams, with right sides facing. Baste two attached SHOE sections together and stitch upper curved edges. Turn to right side and topstitch close to edge.

B. Stitch two layers of SOLE to each shoe, with right sides facing and notches matching seams. Turn the shoe right side out.

C. Fold T-STRAP in half and stitch 1 inch from fold, as shown on pattern. Pin front point of shoe over the curved end of T-strap and stitch together. Glue the two layers of ANKLE STRAP together. Pin the back edge of shoe over the outside pointed corner of the strap and stitch strap to shoe.

D. Place shoes on doll. Insert the long end of the strap through the opening in the T-strap. Fasten ends of strap together by stitching through a small button.

The Baby Doll

The baby doll is called Wendy, my first baby's name. This Wendy is as delicate as her namesake. Her dress and bloomer panties are made of ivory eyelet, and the ruffles on the dress are cut from the scalloped border of the eyelet fabric. The dress could be made of any pastel cotton.

Pattern Pieces for Baby Doll (see pages 123 through 129)

BODY FRONT (1), BODY BACK (1), ARM (4), LEG (4) from BODY fabric

HAIR FRONT (1), HAIR BACK (1), BOW (46) from HAIR fabric

EYE (2) from EYE fabric

CHEEK (2) from CHEEK fabric

Materials Required for Baby

BODY fabric, ⅜ yard of unbleached muslin

HAIR fabric, ⅜ yard of orange cotton

EYE fabric, black felt scrap

CHEEK fabric, bright pink felt scrap

MOUTH, bright pink six-strand embroidery thread

Making the Doll

Cut out all pieces.

STEP 1. MAKING THE BODY FRONT

A. Use three strands of six-strand embroidery cotton in needle to work the MOUTH. Work mouth on BODY FRONT in pink, with a satin stitch.

B. Baste HAIR FRONT to the body front, with right sides facing, matching center notches. Baste or pin and stitch at the center notch and sew each side to neck from this center point so hair will be centered on face. Carefully clip the hair front seam allowances, and press them toward the hair front.

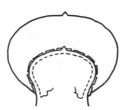

STEP 2. MAKING THE ARMS AND LEGS

A. Pin ARM sections together, with right sides facing. Stitch, leaving the straight edge open. Carefully clip to the inward corner and turn the arm right side out. Stuff the arm firmly and baste the opening closed.

B. Baste arms to the right side of the body front, with the thumbs down, and matching the notches.

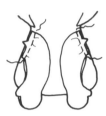

C. Stitch LEG sections together, with right sides facing. Stitch, leaving the straight edge open. Carefully clip to the inward curves and turn the legs right side out. Stuff the legs and baste the opening closed.

D. Baste legs to the lower edge of body front, with legs facing right side of body, then machine-stitch.

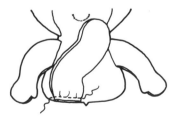

STEP 3. ASSEMBLING THE BODY

A. Stitch HAIR BACK to BODY BACK, with right sides facing and notches matching.

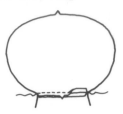

B. Baste the body back to the body front, with right sides facing. Stitch, keeping the arms and legs tucked into body and leaving the bottom open.

C. Carefully clip the inward curves and turn the body right side out. Stuff the body firmly and sew the opening closed.

STEP 4. FINISHING THE HAIR AND FACE

A. Glue EYES and CHEEKS to the face.

B. Cut forty-six hair bows, each 1½ inches by 2¾ inches. Pink outer edges of bows with pinking shears. Gather and wrap thread around bows. Complete forty-six bows. Pin bows to the doll's hair, distribute them evenly, and sew in place by hand at center of bow.

Pattern Pieces for Baby's Clothes (see pages 123 through 129)

DRESS (2) cut a rectangular pattern, 6½ by 12 inches, and cut a rectangular pattern (2), 8 by 12 inches, PANTIES (2) cut a rectangular pattern 6 by 12 inches, from DRESS fabric
SHOE (8), ANKLE STRAP (4) from SHOE felt

Materials Required for Baby's Clothes

DRESS fabric, ⅜ yard of ivory eyelet cotton with scalloped border, or pastel cotton
SHOE fabric, 9 by 18 inches of pale pink felt
Dress trim, ⅓ yard of ¾- to 1-inch-wide pale pink moire ribbon
Shoe trim, two ⅜-inch white buttons
Elastic, 1⅓ yards of ¼-inch width

Making the Clothes

Cut out all pieces.

STEP 1. MAKING THE DRESS

A. For dress, use four rectangles (two for front, two for back), two 6½ inches long and 12 inches wide and another two 8 inches long and 12 inches wide. Baste the shorter pieces over the longer ones, and treat the double layers as one, using scalloped edge for hems.

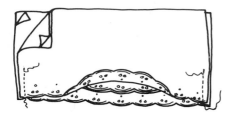

B. Pin the front to the back, with right sides facing. Stitch the sides, leaving a 5-inch opening above stitching for armholes. Turn in ¼ inch on armhole edges and machine-stitch.

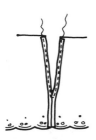

C. Turn down 2 inches at dress neck edge to form ruffle. Turn under ¼ inch on the raw edge and stitch in place. Stitch ⅜ inch above this stitching to form casing. Run ¼-inch-wide (or narrower) elastic through casings, place the dress on the doll, and draw up the elastic to form the ruffle. Secure the elastic ends together and tuck them inside dress.

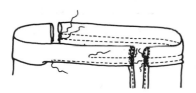

D. Pin ¾- to 1-inch-wide trim to the right side of the dress neck edge. Turn in one end at one side seam and sew in place by hand.

E. Tie ribbon into a double bow and sew to front neck. Trim the ends of ribbon.

STEP 2. MAKING THE PANTIES

A. Make the panties, following the directions for Brenda Sue's panties.

STEP 3. MAKING THE SHOES

A. Pin four groups of 2 SHOE sections together and stitch the inward curved edge. Carefully clip the curve, turn right side out, and topstitch edge. Pin two of these SHOE sections together to make each of two shoes, and stitch the seam.

B. Turn the shoe right side out. Glue the two layers of ANKLE STRAP together. Pin the back edges of shoe over the outside pointed corner on the strap and stitch together.

C. Place shoes on doll. Fasten ends of strap together with small buttons.

CHAPTER 7

Pillows, Pajama Bags, and Pot Holders

This chapter contains a variety of dolls that are decorative accessories—a pajama bag, three pillows, and a set of pot holders. The construction of the Gingham Pajama-Bag Doll is similar to that of the Rag Doll Family in Chapter 6. The French Sailor Pillow-Doll is similar in construction to the Three Working Men in Chapter 3. The patterns for the three men could also be enlarged to make decorative pillows.

The Flying Angel Pillow-Doll has a different form of construction and so do the pot-holder dolls, while the Cupid Pillow-Doll is the only project in the book that is made entirely of felt. It is topstitched at every seam, so no turning of the fabric is required. This makes it one of the easiest projects in the book.

Cupid Pillow-Doll

My Cupid Pillow-Doll, Valentin, hands you his heart. This pillow is quite simple to make. The various elements are topstitched, stuffed, and closed, then assembled and sewn together by hand. Finally, the features are glued on. The Cupid Pillow-Doll would be a wonderful present to give someone you love. Its measurements are approximately 10 by 23 inches.

Pattern Pieces (see pages 130 through 132)

WING (2) from WING fabric
HAIR FRONT (1), HAIR BACK (1), LARGE HAIR CIRCLE (20), MEDIUM HAIR CIRCLE (12), SMALL HAIR CIRCLE (4), from HAIR fabric
FACE (1), ARM (4) from FACE fabric
HEART (2) from HEART fabric
EYE (2) from EYE fabric
CHEEK (2), MOUTH (1) from CHEEK fabric

Materials Required

WING fabric, ⅜ yard of white 72-inch-wide felt
HAIR fabric, ¼ yard of chestnut brown 72-inch-wide felt
FACE fabric, 9 by 25 inches of flesh-tone felt
HEART fabric, 9 by 3 inches of magenta felt
EYE fabric, black felt scrap
CHEEK fabric, bright pink felt scrap

Making the Pillow-Doll

Cut out all pieces.

STEP 1. MAKING THE WINGS

A. Pin WINGS together, with the raw edges even, right side out. Stitch ¼ inch from the raw edges, leaving an opening for stuffing. Stitch again ¼ inch from the first row of stitching.

B. Stuff the wings firmly and stitch the opening closed.

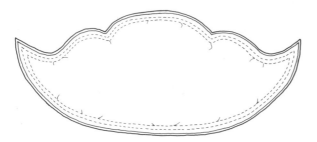

STEP 2. MAKING THE FACE AND HAIR

A. Pin FACE ¼ inch over the raw edge of HAIR FRONT. Stitch face in place close to the outer edge.

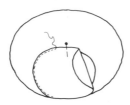

B. Pin the face and hair front to HAIR BACK, with raw edges even, right side out. Stitch close to the raw edges, leaving an opening.

C. Stuff the face and hair lightly and stitch the openings closed.

D. Pin two layers of small, medium, and large HAIR circles together, with the raw edges even and right sides out. There are eighteen double layers of hair altogether—two small, six medium, and ten large circles. Stitch close to the raw edges.

E. Pin hair circles to hair front, with the smaller circles at the bottom, working up to the larger circles at top of hair. Have the circles overlap at the face line. With the circles overlapping each other, sew them securely in place.

F. Place the hair and face on the wings at the center, with the upper edges even. Sew securely in place.

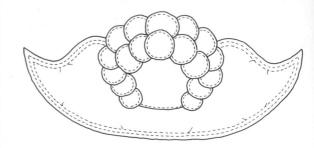

STEP 3. MAKING THE ARMS

A. Pin two layers of ARM together, with the raw edges even, right sides out. Stitch close to the raw edges, leaving an opening. Repeat for second arm.

B. Stuff the arms lightly and stitch the openings closed.

C. Pin arms to the wings, just covering the lower edge of the face, lapping right arm over left, as shown. Stitch the arms securely in place.

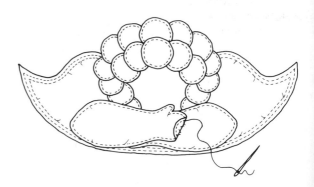

STEP 4. FINISHING THE PILLOW

A. Pin the two layers of HEART together, with the raw edges even, right sides out. Stitch close to the raw edges.

B. Place heart between the thumb and right hand. Sew heart securely in place.

C. Glue EYES, CHEEKS, and MOUTH to face.

Flying Angel Pillow-Doll

My Mother has always been an angel to me, so I have named my pillow Lillian, after her. Lillian is made of a white heavy-weight cotton canvas trimmed with very full eyelet ruffles and eyelet beading. Red-and-white gingham ribbon is pulled through the eyelet beading and used for a bow in the Angel's hair. The pillow could be made of a medium- to heavy-weight cotton in a solid, stripe, or print, or in a cotton velveteen, and it can be made to harmonize with almost any color scheme by simply changing the color of the ribbon trim. If you prefer to make a boy angel, place the ribbon bow under the chin, instead of in the hair. A pair of Angels, a boy and a girl, would be a wonderful holiday decoration. It measures 19 by 9 inches.

Pattern Pieces (see pages 133 through 135)

BODY (2), FRONT SLEEVE (1), BACK SLEEVE (1), WING (2) from BODY fabric
FACE (1), HAND (2), FOOT (2) from FACE fabric
HAIR FRONT (1), HAIR BACK (1), YO-YO (10) from HAIR fabric
EYE (2) from EYE fabric
CHEEK (2) from CHEEK fabric

Materials Required

BODY fabric, ½ yard of white cotton canvas
FACE fabric, 9 by 14 inches of flesh-toned cotton
HAIR fabric, ¼ yard of brown cotton
EYE fabric, black felt scrap
CHEEK fabric, bright pink felt scrap
MOUTH, red six-strand embroidery thread
Dress trim, 5 yards of 3-inch-wide eyelet edging, 1 yard of 1-inch-wide eyelet beading, 1¼ yards of 1-inch-wide red-and-white gingham ribbon

Making the Pillow-Doll

Cut out all pieces.

STEP 1. MAKING THE HANDS AND SLEEVES

A. Fold each HAND in half, with right sides facing. Stitch the curved edges together. Turn the hands right side out, stuff them lightly, and baste the raw edges together.

B. Baste a hand to the right side of each SLEEVE, matching the double notches.

C. Fold the front and back sleeves in half, with right sides facing. Stitch, leaving the slanted edge open. Turn the sleeves right side out, stuff them lightly, and baste the raw edges together.

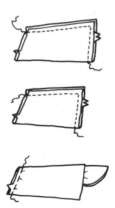

D. Baste the front sleeve to the back sleeve, matching notches. Baste sleeves to the right side of one BODY section, with the notches matching and the front sleeve against the body.

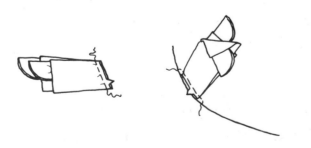

STEP 2. ASSEMBLING THE BODY

A. Pin the remaining BODY section to the body, with right sides facing. Stitch, leaving the short straight edge open and leaving an opening on the curved edge.

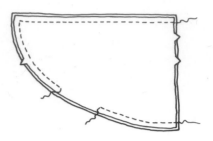

B. Use 3 yards of scalloped eyelet for the body ruffle. Cut the eyelet in half. Stitch the short ends of each half together to form two eyelet rings. Baste the rings together, with one scalloped edge ½ inch from the other scalloped edge. Run a gathering stitch along the straight edge on the eyelet layers to form a double ruffle.

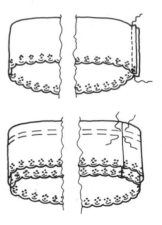

C. Pin the ruffle to the right side of the back edge of the body, with the narrower ruffle against the body. Narrower ruffle should have 2¼ inches showing, and wider ruffle should have 2¾ inches showing at edge of dress. Pull up the gathers to fit and baste.

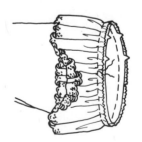

D. Fold each FOOT in half, with right sides facing, and stitch the curved edges. Turn each foot right side out, stuff it, and baste the raw edges together.

E. Baste the feet to the right side of the body, with the notches matching.

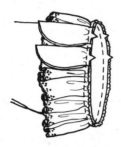

F. Stitch the body bottom closed, with ruffles and feet inside. Turn the body right side out through the curved opening, stuff it firmly, and sew the opening closed by hand.

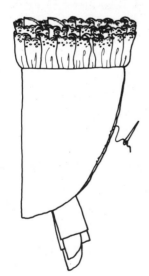

STEP 3. MAKING THE HEAD

A. Use three strands of six-strand embroidery cotton when stitching the mouth. Work mouth on FACE in red with a satin stitch.

B. Baste face to HAIR FRONT, with right sides facing, matching center notches. Stitch. Carefully clip the hair front seam allowances and press seam allowances toward the hair front.

C. Pin HAIR BACK to the head front, with right sides facing. Stitch, leaving an opening. Turn the head right side out, stuff it lightly, and sew the opening closed.

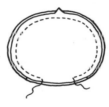 

D. Using a double strand of thread in needle, turn in ¼ inch on a raw edges of YO-YO and hand-gather around the entire edge. Pull up the thread tightly and adjust the gathers. Knot the thread ends securely. Complete ten yo-yo's. Pin yo-yo's to hair front, distributing them so they overlap the hair seams. Sew in place by hand.

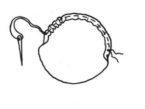 

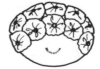

E. Use 2 yards of scalloped eyelet for head ruffle. Stitch the short ends together and run a gathering stitch along the straight edge.

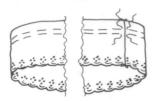

F. Pin the ruffle to the hair back. Allow 2 inches of the ruffle width to show. Pull up the gathers to fit, as shown in the drawing, and sew securely in place by hand. Cover the raw edges with eyelet beading and sew beading in place.

G. Pin the head to the body front, as shown, and sew in place.

STEP 4. FINISHING THE ANGEL

A. Insert ribbon through openings in the beading. Pin beading to the right side of body along the back ruffled seam, and sew in place.

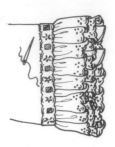

B. Pin WINGS sections together, with right sides facing. Stitch, leaving an opening.

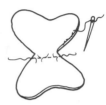

C. Carefully clip to the inward curves. Turn wings right side out, stuff them, and sew the opening closed. Stitch wings along the dashed line.

D. Fold the wings along the stitching and sew them to the top of the body by hand, with the shorter wing in front.

E. Glue EYES and CHEEKS to the face, as shown.

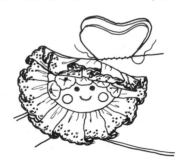

F. Tie the ribbon into a bow and sew it to bottom of face for a boy angel or to the hair yo-yos for a girl angel. Trim the ends of the ribbon.

Girl   Boy

HAIR FRONT (1), HAIR BACK (1), HAIR BOWS (40) cut a
    rectangular pattern, 6 by 1¾ inches, from HAIR
    fabric
FACE (1), ARM (4) from FACE fabric
BODY (2), DRESS (2) cut a square pattern, 18 by 18
    inches, DRESS RUFFLE (2) cut a rectangular pat-
    tern, 5 by 36 inches, LARGE HAIR BOW (1) cut a
    rectangular pattern, 2½ by 16 inches, KNOT (1) cut
    a square pattern, 3 by 3 inches, of DRESS fabric
EYE (2) from EYE fabric
CHEEK (2) from CHEEK fabric

Materials Required

HAIR fabric, ½ yard of orange cotton
FACE fabric, 9 by 19 inches of flesh-toned cotton
DRESS fabric, 1⅛ yards of pink-and-white gingham
EYE fabric, black felt scrap
CHEEK fabric, bright pink felt scrap
MOUTH, bright pink embroidery thread
Dress trim, 1½ yards of 1-inch-wide eyelet beading,
    1½ yards of ½-inch-wide pale pink satin ribbon
Skirt closing (optional), ⅓ yard of self-gripping fas-
    tener
Stuffing, polyester fiber filling
Heavy string, ½ yard

Making the Pajama-Bag Doll

Cut out all pieces.

Gingham Pajama-Bag Doll

This pretty gingham doll is meant to sit on a bed. Her
name is Nancy Ann, and she was made to hold pa-
jamas under her skirt. Nancy Ann's distinguishing feature is her hair, which is constructed of bows made
from strips of orange cotton fabric. She would make
an excellent project for a mother and daughter to
make together because her dress is extremely simple
to sew. Mother could sew and stuff the doll form, and
daughter could be taught to make the dress and bows
for her hair. It would be a good idea to use a light- to
medium-weight cotton fabric that harmonizes with
the room in which she will sit. The finished doll will
be approximately 24 inches tall.

STEP 1. MAKING THE BODY FRONT AND BACK

A. Use three strands of six-strand embroidery cotton
in needle to work the mouth. Work mouth on FACE in
pink, with a satin stitch.

B. Baste face to HAIR FRONT, with right sides facing and center notches matching. Baste or pin and stitch at the center notch, and sew each side to neck from this center point so that hair will be centered on face. Carefully clip the hair front seam allowances and press seam allowances toward the hair front.

C. Pin the head front to one BODY section, with right sides facing. Match the notches and stitch the neck seam; then press the seam toward the body section.

D. Pin HAIR BACK to remaining BODY section with right sides facing. Match the notches and stitch the neck seam; then press the seam toward the body section.

STEP 2. MAKING THE ARMS AND BODY SEAM

A. Pin ARM sections together, with right sides facing. Stitch, leaving the straight edge open. Carefully clip to the inward corners and turn the arm right side out. Stuff the arm firmly, leaving space at the tops, and baste the opening closed.

B. Baste arms to the right side of the body front, with the thumbs down and matching the notches.

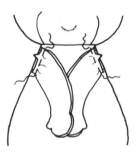

C. Baste the body back to the body front, with right sides facing. Stitch, keeping the arms tucked into the body and leaving an opening at the bottom.

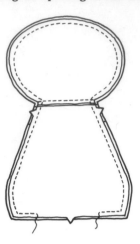

D. Carefully clip the inward corners and turn the body right side out. Stuff the body firmly and sew the opening closed.

STEP 3. MAKING THE DRESS

A. For the dress, use the two squares, one for front and one for back, each 18 inches long and 18 inches wide. Pin the front to the back, with right sides facing. Leaving an 8-inch opening for the armholes, stitch the sides. Turn under ¼ inch on armhole edges and machine-stitch.

B. For ruffle use the two rectangles, each 5 inches long and 36 inches wide. Pin the ruffle pieces together, with right sides facing. Stitch the short sides. Run a gathering stitch along the top of the ruffle. Turn under ¼ inch on bottom edge of ruffle and machine-stitch.

C. With right sides facing, pin the ruffle to the bottom of the dress, matching the side seams and pulling up gathers to fit dress. Stitch the seam. Press the seam allowances toward the dress.

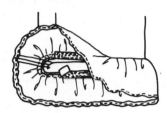

D. If you wish to make the doll into a pajama bag, sew a 12-inch-long self-gripping fastener to the wrong side of the lower edge of dress, by hand.

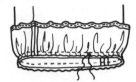

E. Insert ribbon through openings in the eyelet beading. Pin beading to the right side of the dress at lower edge above ruffle. Turn in one raw end at one side seam and sew the beading in place by hand. The remaining beading will be used over the neck ruffle.

F. Turn down 2¼ inches at dress neck edge to form ruffle. Turn under ¼ inch on the raw edge and stitch in place. Stitch ½ inch above this stitching to form a casing. Run a string through this casing, using a small safety pin to pull the string through.

G. Place the dress on the doll and draw up the string to form the ruffle. Knot the string and tuck the loose ends inside the dress. Pin the beading to the right side of the dress neck edge. Turn in one raw end at one side seam and sew the beading in place by hand.

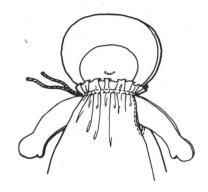

STEP 4. FINISHING THE DOLL

A. Apply EYES and CHEEKS to the face with glue.

B. Use the forty hair bows, each 6 inches by 1¾ inches. Turn in ¼ inch on the long edges and machine-stitch. Fold each piece in half, with right sides facing. Stitch the short ends. Turn each bow right side out, bring the seam to the center, and gather and wrap thread around the center of the bow. Complete all forty bows. Pin the bows to the hair front and back, distributing them evenly, and sew in place by hand.

C. For the large hair bow, use the rectangle 16 inches by 2½ inches. Turn in ¼ inch on all edges and machine-stitch. Fold the rectangle, as shown, and tack the center of the bow securely.

D. For the knot, use the square 3 inches by 3 inches. Fold the raw ends back, wrap it around the center of the bow, and sew the edges together at the back of the bow. Sew the large bow to the head by hand.

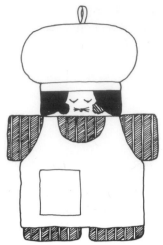

Two Chefs Pot-Holder Dolls

Virginia and Vicente are two chefs created to hang on your kitchen wall. They are working pot holders and are completely washable, and, if you make them of no-iron cotton, they will come out of the dryer ready to use. These pot holders are constructed very much like dolls, however, unlike dolls, they are flat, because they are filled with batting, instead of with stuffing.

Dress these pot-holder dolls in a color that harmonizes with your kitchen and enjoy them as decorative accents. Both chef's are 11 inches tall.

Pattern Pieces for Each (see pages 138 through 139)

BODY (2) of BODY fabric
HAT (2), HATBAND (2), LOOP (1) cut a rectangular pattern 1 by 1½ inches, APRON FRONT (1), APRON BACK (1), POCKET (1), STRAP (2) from HAT fabric
FACE (1) from FACE fabric
HAIR FRONT (4), HAIR BACK (1), YO-YO (woman only) (4) from HAIR fabric

Materials Required for Each

BODY fabric, 9 by 20 inches of red pin-dot cotton for woman, red with white stripe cotton for man
HAT fabric, 9 by 30 inches of white cotton
FACE fabric, 4 by 5 inches of flesh-toned cotton
HAIR fabric, for woman, 9 by 12 inches of dark brown cotton, for man, 9 by 5 inches of dark brown cotton
EYES, black six-strand embroidery floss
MOUTH, red six-strand embroidery floss
CHEEKS, pink six-strand embroidery threads
Apron trim for woman, ½ yard of ¾-inch-wide pregathered eyelet ruffling
Apron back trim, two ½-inch white shirt buttons
Stuffing, quilt batting

Making the Pot-Holder Dolls

Cut out all pieces.

STEP 1. MAKING THE HEAD FRONT

A. Baste FACE over lower part of one HAT section, with right sides up and bottom edges even.

B. Use three strands of embroidery floss in needle when embroidering the features. Stitch cheeks in pink with a satin stitch. Work lips in red with two straight horizontal stitches and two slanting vertical stitches at center for the woman, as shown. Work eyes in black with an open lazy daisy stitch, as shown. Make the man's mustache by knotting twelve strands of black embroidery floss together. Trim the mustache to ⅜ inch on each side of knot and tack the knot to face above lips.

C. Pin each pair of HAIR FRONT sections together, with right sides facing, and stitch together along the curved edge. Turn each one right side out and baste the raw edges together. Press. Baste the hair front sections over the face, as shown in the drawing, and stitch close to the upper and side edges.

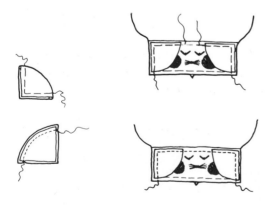

D. Pin one long edge of HATBAND to the right side of HAT FRONT, making the raw edge even with the top edge of hair and face. Stitch from A to B, ¼ inch from

raw edge. Turn the band down and press. Turn under the remaining long edge and sew it in place by hand, covering the raw edges.

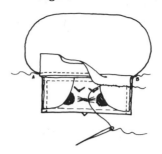

STEP 2. MAKING THE BODY FRONT

A. Turn neck and armhole edges of APRON FRONT under ¼ inch. Stitch close to the turned edges.

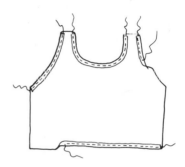

B. Turn POCKET down ½ inch from top and baste. Turn in ¼ inch on remaining three sides and baste. Pin pocket to the apron front, as shown, and stitch close to the sides and lower edges.

C. With right sides up, baste the apron to one BODY section.

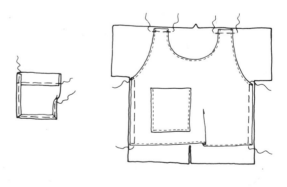

D. With right sides facing, pin the head front to the body front, matching the notches. Stitch the neck seam, then press the seam open.

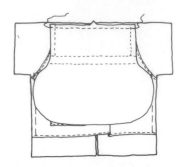

STEP 3. MAKING THE HEAD BACK

A. Baste HAIR over lower part of remaining HAT section, with right sides up and raw edges even. Stitch close to the upper and side edges of hair.

B. Pin one long edge of HATBAND to the right side of hat back, making the raw edge even with the top edge of hair. Stitch from A to B ¼ inch from raw edge. Turn the band down and press. Turn under the remaining long edge and sew it in place by hand, covering the raw edges.

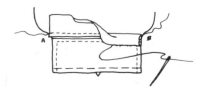

C. For loop, use a piece of white fabric 1½ inches long and 1 inch wide. Turn in ¼ inch on long edges. Bring these edges together and press, or cut a piece of double-fold bias tape 1½ inches long. Stitch folded edges together. Fold loop in half and baste it to the hat back at center, as shown in the drawing.

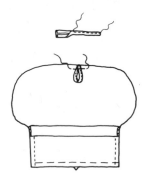

STEP 4. MAKING THE BODY BACK

A. Turn in ¼ inch on long edges of each STRAP and stitch close to the turned edges. Baste straps to re-

maining BODY section, with right sides up, making a 1¼-inch space at center and crossing straps as shown. Trim straps as shown.

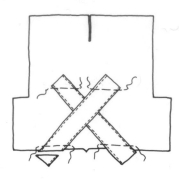

B. Turn in ¼ inch on long edges of APRON BACK. Stitch close to the turned edges. Baste apron back to body back at the same level as on the body front, with right sides up. Sew two ½-inch buttons to apron back at ends of straps through all layers.

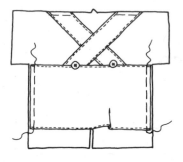

C. Pin the head back to the body back with right sides facing. Match the notches and stitch the neck seam, then press the seam open.

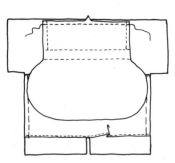

STEP 5. ASSEMBLING THE BODY

A. Baste the entire front to two layers of quilt batting.

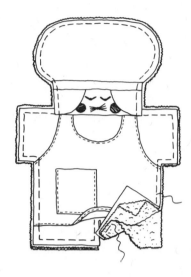

B. With right sides facing, baste the back to the front. Stitch, being careful not to catch lower edge of apron while stitching, and leaving an opening for turning. Stitch again over the inward corners to reinforce them. Carefully clip to the inward corners, trim the outward corners, and turn the body right side out.

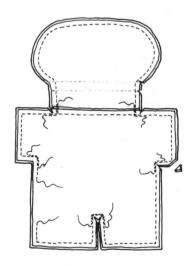

C. Sew the opening closed. Hand-quilt by taking tiny running stitches along the top of the hatband, along the neckline, the arms, and the top of the legs under the apron, following along the apron front. The male chef is now complete.

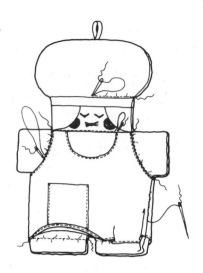

STEP 6. FINISHING THE WOMAN

A. Using a double strand of thread in needle, turn in ¼ inch on raw edges of YO-YO and hand-gather around the entire edge. Pull up the thread tightly and adjust the gathers. Knot the thread ends securely. Complete four yo-yo's and sew to back hair, as shown in the drawing.

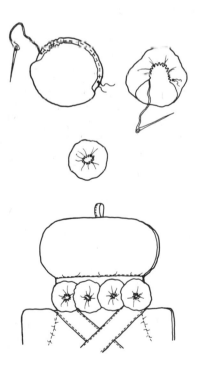

B. Sew eyelet ruffling by hand ½ inch above lower edge of apron.

French Sailor Pillow-Doll

Pierre the French Sailor is quite easy to sew and would look particularly appealing as a decorative pillow in a den, playroom, or little boy's room. The construction is simply done by sewing all of the details to his body front, and then sewing the completed front to the body back. When he is turned and stuffed, he is complete. Pierre measures 24 by 14 inches.

Pattern Pieces (see pages 140 through 143)

BODY (2), SLEEVE (2), HAT (2) from BODY fabric
HATBAND (1), POM-PON (1), COLLAR (4), KNOT (1) from COLLAR fabric
FRONT INSET (1) of INSET fabric
FACE (2), HAND (4) from FACE fabric
BOOT (2), EYE (2), MUSTACHE (1), SIDEBURN (2) from BOOT fabric

Materials Required

BODY fabric, ¾ yard of navy blue cotton
COLLAR fabric, 9 by 30 inches of red velveteen
INSET fabric, 6 by 6 inches of black-and-white striped denim ticking
FACE fabric, 9 by 16 inches of white felt
BOOT fabric, 9 by 10 inches of black felt
Sleeve trim, 1 yard of ¼-inch-wide red velvet ribbon
Stuffing, polyester fiber filling

Making the Pillow-Doll

Cut out all pieces.

STEP 1. MAKING THE BODY FRONT

A. Pin FRONT INSET to the right side of one BODY section at the dotted line position, and stitch close to the outer edges.

B. Baste the two layers of FACE together, with the raw edges even. Pin the face to the right side of body front at the dotted line position, and stitch close to the outer edges.

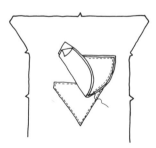

C. Pin SIDEBURNS and MUSTACHE to the face, as shown in the drawing, and stitch in place close to the outer edges.

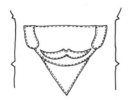

STEP 2. MAKING THE HAT, BAND, AND COLLAR

A. Turn under long edges of HATBAND ¼ inch and baste. Pin the hatband to the body front, with half of the band overlapping the upper edge of the face. Sew the band in place by hand with tiny stitches.

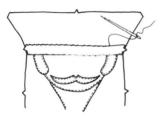

B. Pin HAT sections together, with right sides facing, and stitch along the curved edge. Turn the hat right side out, and baste the raw edges together.

C. Baste the hat to the upper edge of the body front, matching the notches.

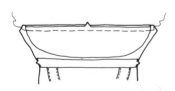

D. Fold POM-PON in half, with the right sides facing, and stitch ends. Turn the pom-pon right side out and press. Baste pom-pon to the center of the hat, matching notches.

E. Pin COLLAR sections together, with right sides facing. Stitch, leaving an opening. Trim seams and carefully clip the inward curves. Turn the collars right side out. Press the collars and sew the openings closed.

F. Pin the straight edges of the collars along the side edges of the inset and face, as shown in the drawing. Stitch close to the straight edges, ending at the point of the inset, covering raw edges of inset. Turn collars over the stitching and press.

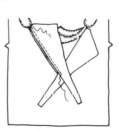

G. Turn under ¼ inch on two edges of KNOT and machine-stitch. Fold knot in half, right sides facing, as shown in the drawing. Stitch seam. Trim and turn right side out with seam to center. Slip the knot around the ends of the collar and sew it securely in place.

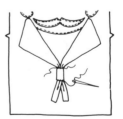

STEP 3. MAKING THE SLEEVES AND BOOTS

A. Sew two rows of ribbon ¾ inch and 1¼ inches above the lower edge of SLEEVE.

B. Glue two layers of HAND together. Baste the hands to the right side of the sleeves, matching the notches.

C. Fold the sleeve in half, with right sides facing. Stitch, leaving the slanted edge open. Turn the sleeve right side out, baste the raw edges together, and press. Baste the sleeves to the right side of body front, matching the notches.

 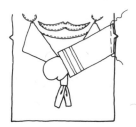

D. With the toes pointing outward, baste BOOTS to the right side of the lower edge of body front, leaving a ¼ inch space between boots. Stitch boots in place.

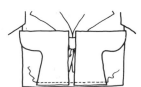

STEP 4. ASSEMBLING THE BODY

A. Baste the remaining BODY section to the body front, with right sides facing. Stitch, keeping the sleeves and boots tucked into the body and leaving an opening at the bottom.

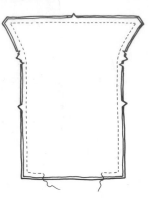

B. Carefully clip the inward curves and turn the body right side out. Stuff it firmly and sew the opening closed.

C. Glue EYES to face, as shown.

Pattern
Pieces

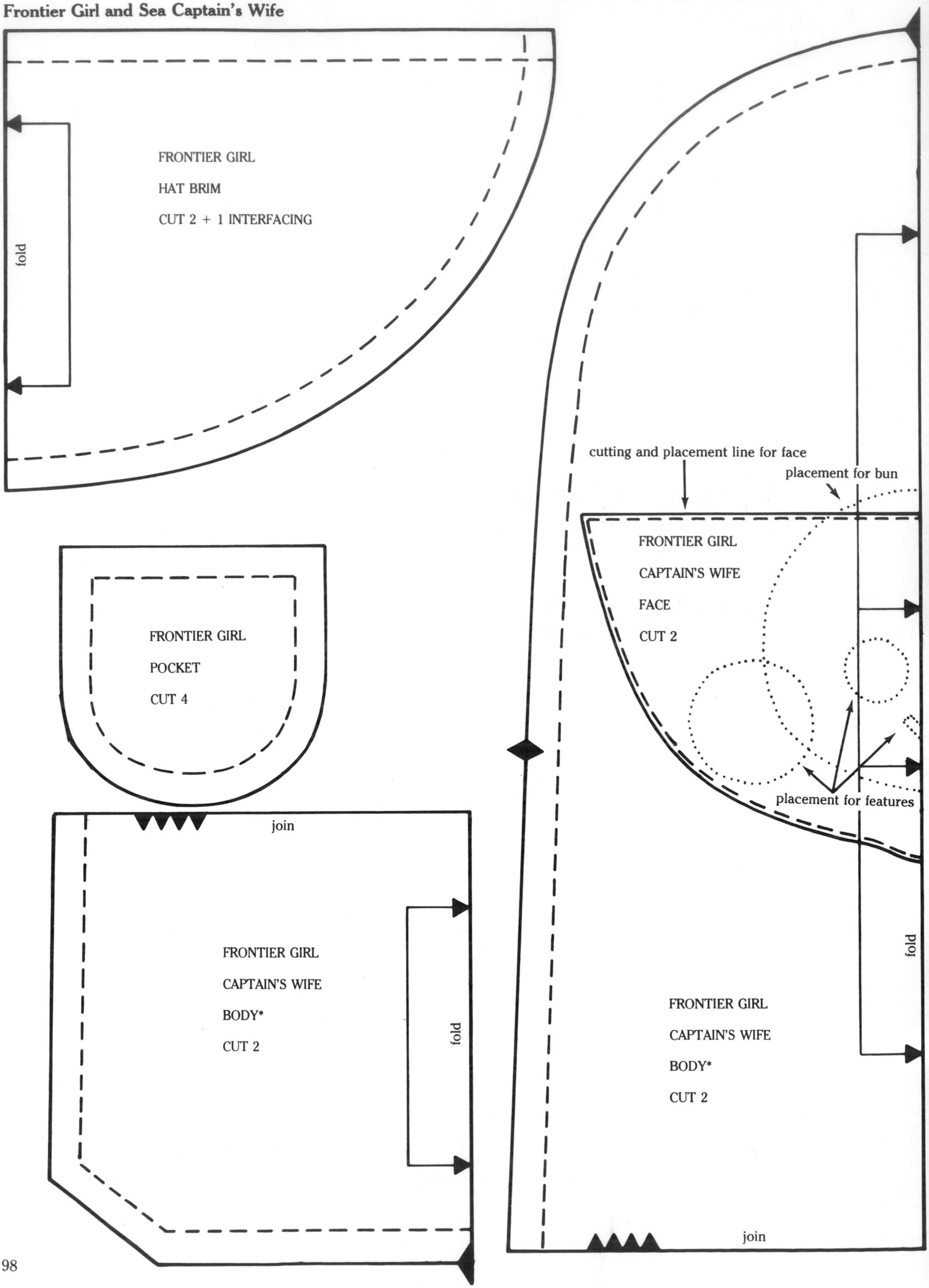

FRONTIER GIRL

HAT BRIM

CUT 2 + 1 INTERFACING

fold

FRONTIER GIRL

POCKET

CUT 4

join

FRONTIER GIRL

CAPTAIN'S WIFE

BODY*

CUT 2

fold

cutting and placement line for face

placement for bun

FRONTIER GIRL

CAPTAIN'S WIFE

FACE

CUT 2

placement for features

fold

FRONTIER GIRL

CAPTAIN'S WIFE

BODY*

CUT 2

join

Frontier Girl, Southern Belle, Sea Captain's Wife

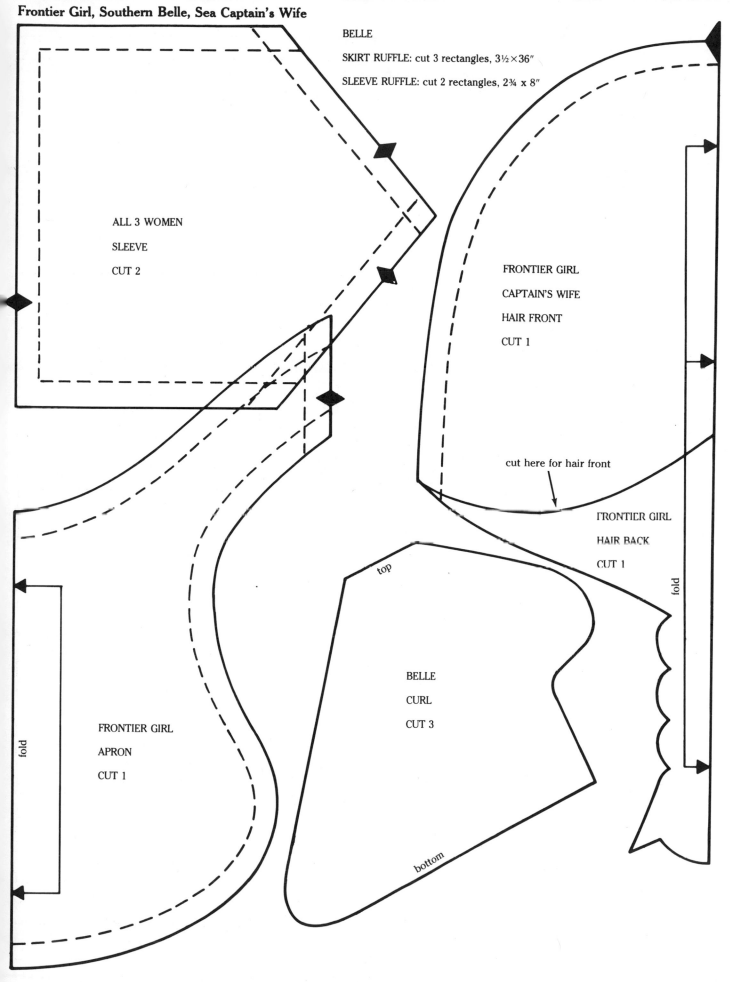

BELLE

SKIRT RUFFLE: cut 3 rectangles, 3½×36"

SLEEVE RUFFLE: cut 2 rectangles, 2¾ x 8"

ALL 3 WOMEN
SLEEVE
CUT 2

FRONTIER GIRL
CAPTAIN'S WIFE
HAIR FRONT
CUT 1

cut here for hair front

FRONTIER GIRL
HAIR BACK
CUT 1

fold

top

FRONTIER GIRL
APRON
CUT 1

fold

BELLE
CURL
CUT 3

bottom

99

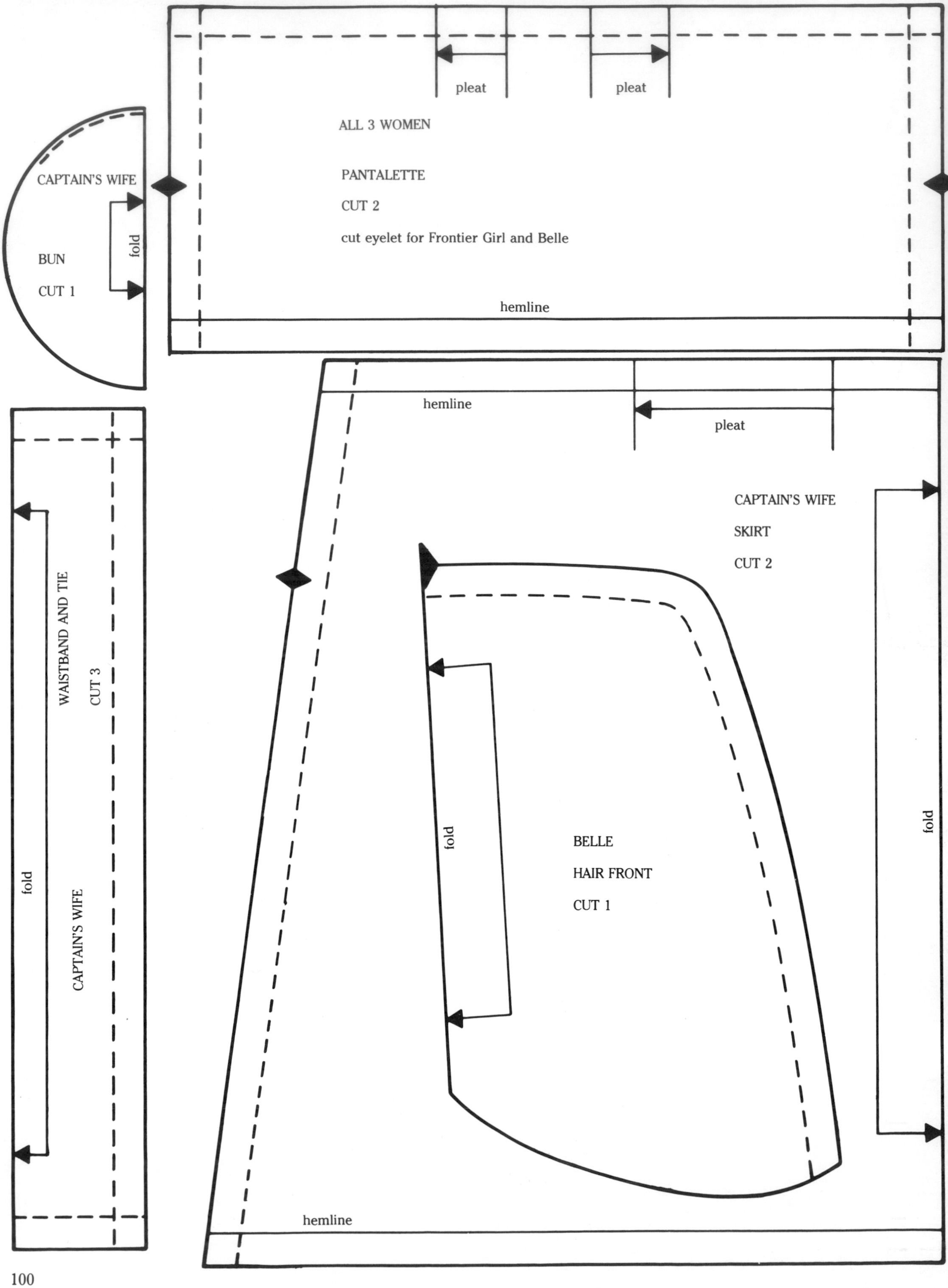

CAPTAIN'S WIFE

BUN

CUT 1

fold

ALL 3 WOMEN

PANTALETTE

CUT 2

cut eyelet for Frontier Girl and Belle

pleat

pleat

hemline

WAISTBAND AND TIE

CUT 3

CAPTAIN'S WIFE

fold

hemline

pleat

CAPTAIN'S WIFE

SKIRT

CUT 2

fold

fold

BELLE

HAIR FRONT

CUT 1

hemline

Frontier Girl, Southern Belle, Sea Captain's Wife

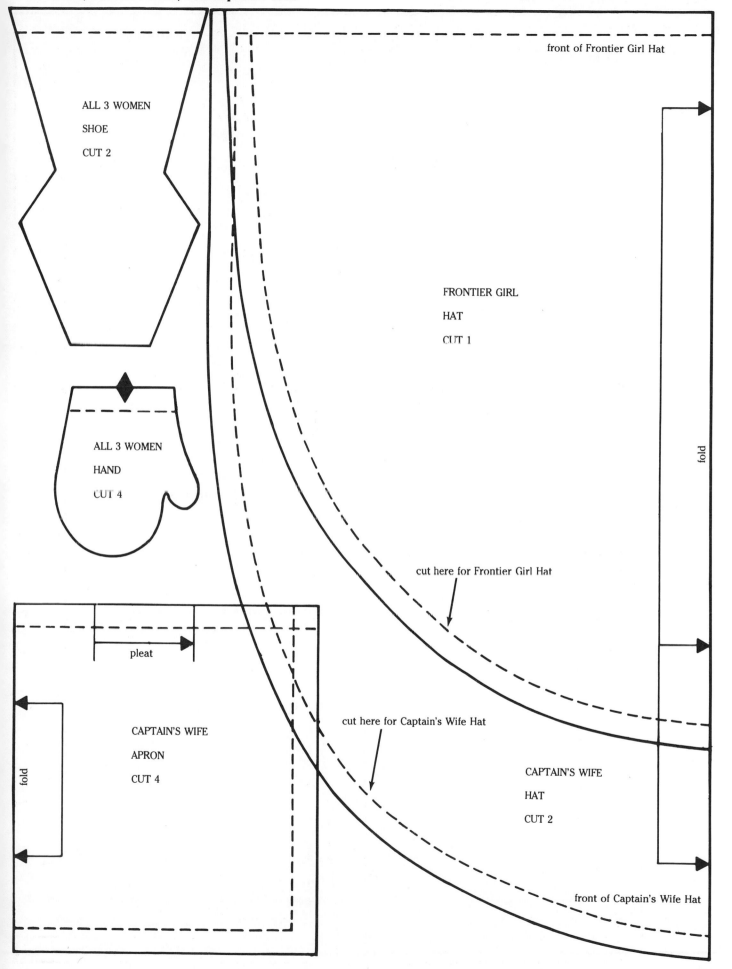

ALL 3 WOMEN
SHOE
CUT 2

ALL 3 WOMEN
HAND
CUT 4

front of Frontier Girl Hat

FRONTIER GIRL
HAT
CUT 1

fold

cut here for Frontier Girl Hat

pleat

cut here for Captain's Wife Hat

CAPTAIN'S WIFE
APRON
CUT 4

fold

CAPTAIN'S WIFE
HAT
CUT 2

front of Captain's Wife Hat

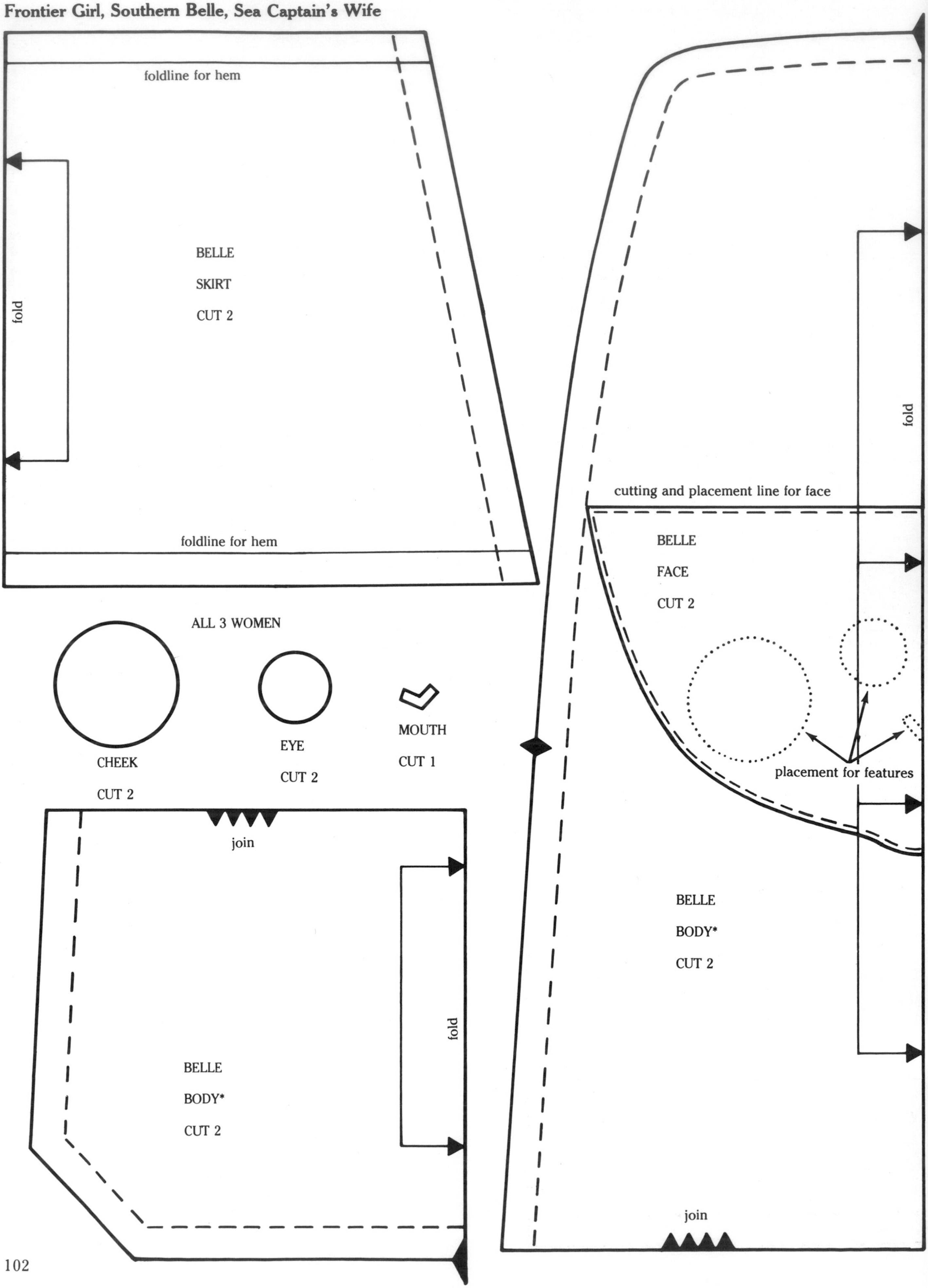

foldline for hem

BELLE

SKIRT

CUT 2

fold

foldline for hem

fold

cutting and placement line for face

BELLE

FACE

CUT 2

ALL 3 WOMEN

CHEEK

CUT 2

EYE

CUT 2

MOUTH

CUT 1

placement for features

join

BELLE

BODY*

CUT 2

fold

BELLE

BODY*

CUT 2

join

Frontier Girl, Southern Belle

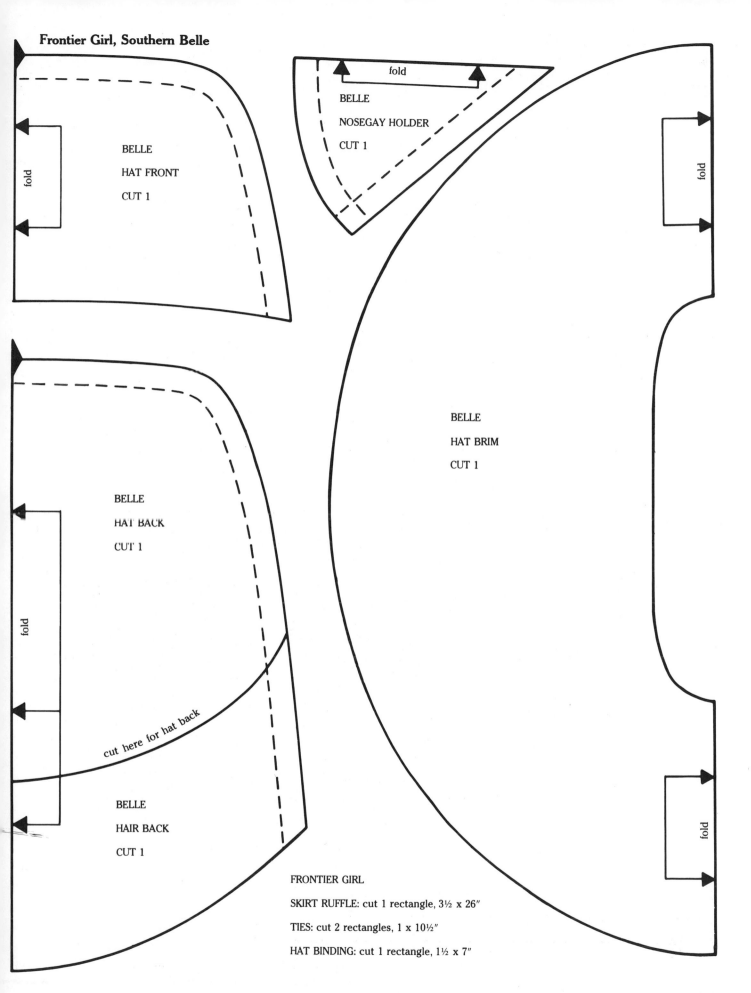

fold

BELLE

NOSEGAY HOLDER

CUT 1

BELLE

HAT FRONT

CUT 1

fold

BELLE

HAT BACK

CUT 1

BELLE

HAT BRIM

CUT 1

fold

fold

cut here for hat back

BELLE

HAIR BACK

CUT 1

FRONTIER GIRL

SKIRT RUFFLE: cut 1 rectangle, 3½ x 26″

TIES: cut 2 rectangles, 1 x 10½″

HAT BINDING: cut 1 rectangle, 1½ x 7″

fold

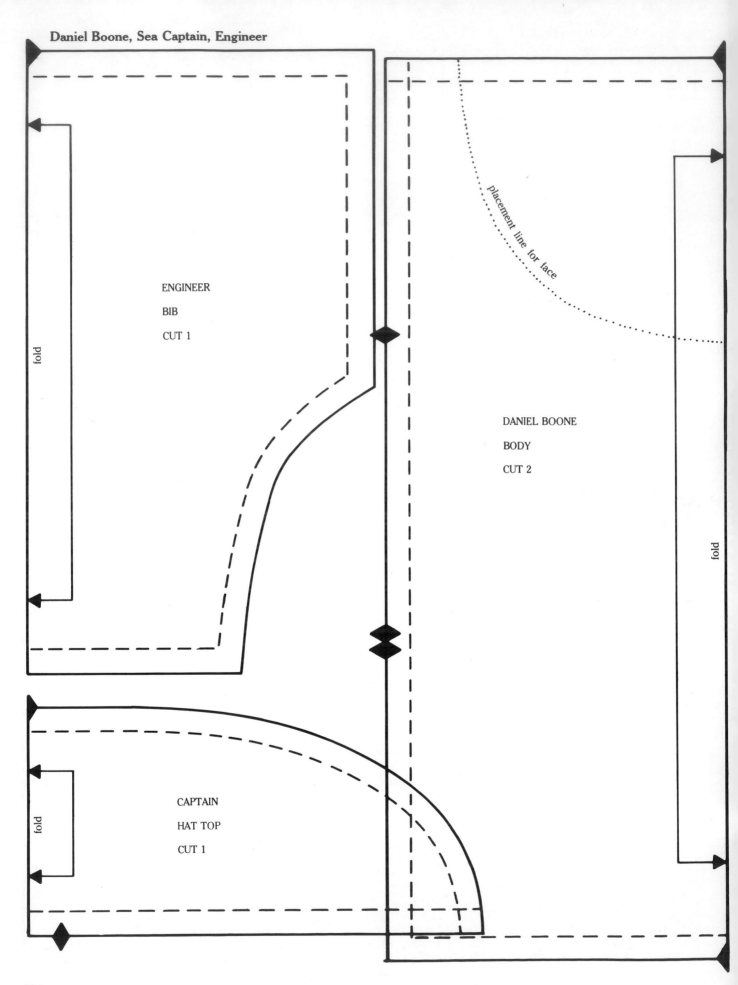

ENGINEER

BIB

CUT 1

fold

DANIEL BOONE

BODY

CUT 2

placement line for face

fold

CAPTAIN

HAT TOP

CUT 1

fold

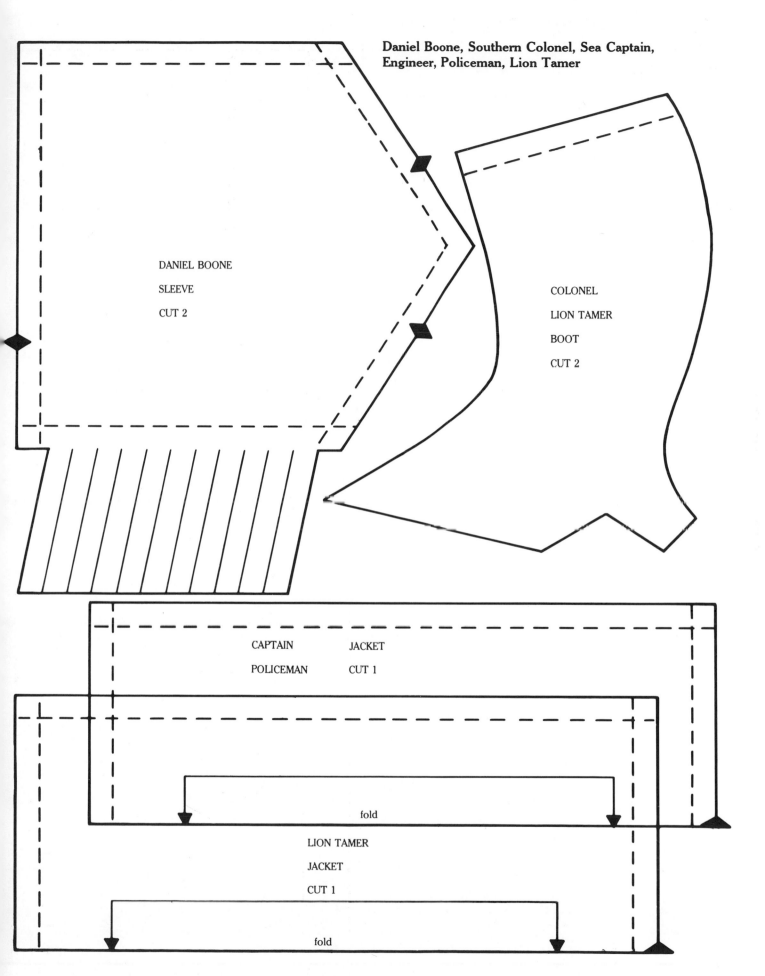

Daniel Boone, Southern Colonel, Sea Captain,
Engineer, Policeman, Lion Tamer

DANIEL BOONE

SLEEVE

CUT 2

COLONEL

LION TAMER

BOOT

CUT 2

CAPTAIN   JACKET

POLICEMAN   CUT 1

fold

LION TAMER

JACKET

CUT 1

fold

Daniel Boone, Sea Captain, Engineer, Policeman,
Lion Tamer

fold

DANIEL BOONE

CAP

CUT 2

CAPTAIN

FACE

CUT 2

fold

placement for features

CUT 1

CAPTAIN   NOSE

ENGINEER

POLICEMAN

LION TAMER

FACE

CUT 2

fold

placement for eye

placement for lower edge of belt

DANIEL BOONE

TUNIC

CUT 1

fold

cut lines for fringe

fold

DANIEL BOONE

HAIR BACK

CUT 1

CAPTAIN

VISOR

CUT 1

fold

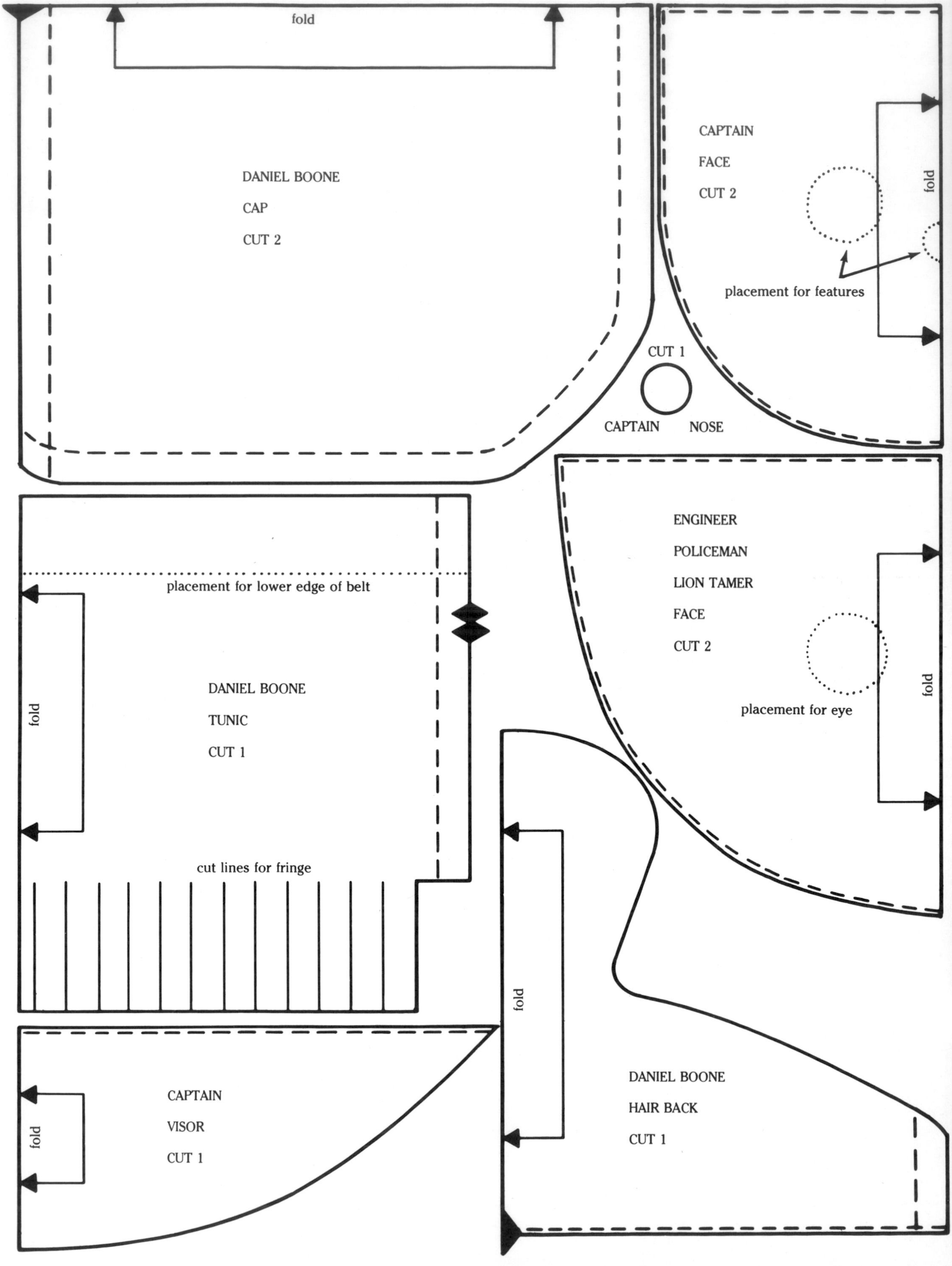

Daniel Boone, Southern Colonel, Sea Captain,
Engineer, Policeman, Lion Tamer

placement for Colonel Braid

placement for Lion Tamer Braid

COLONEL

CAPTAIN

ENGINEER

POLICEMAN

LION TAMER

SLEEVE

CUT 2

COLONEL

SIDEBURN

CUT 2

ALL 6 MEN

HAND

CUT 4

COLONEL

HAIR BACK

CUT 1

COLONEL

JACKET

CUT 2

fold

COLONEL

BELT LEFT FRONT

CUT 1

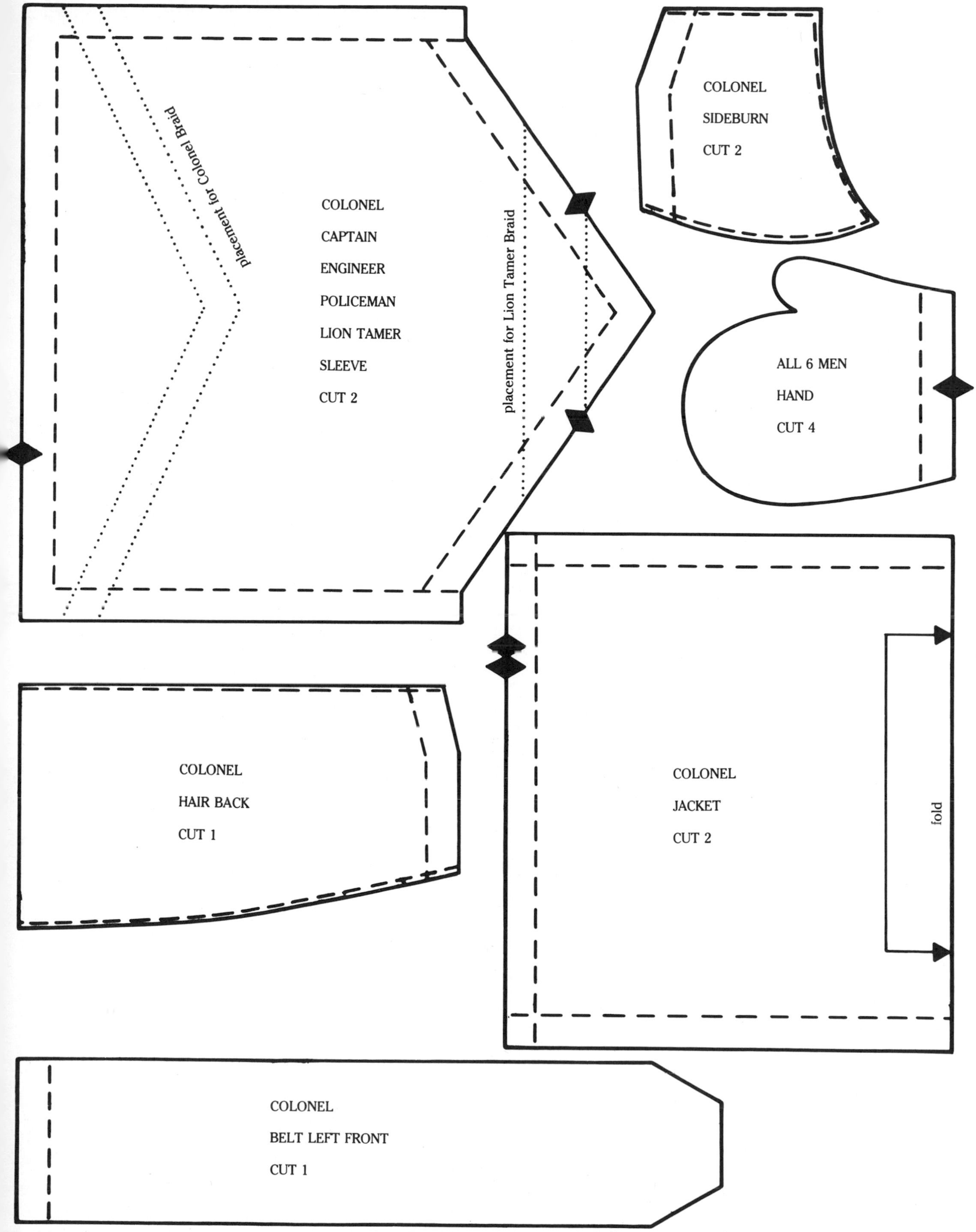

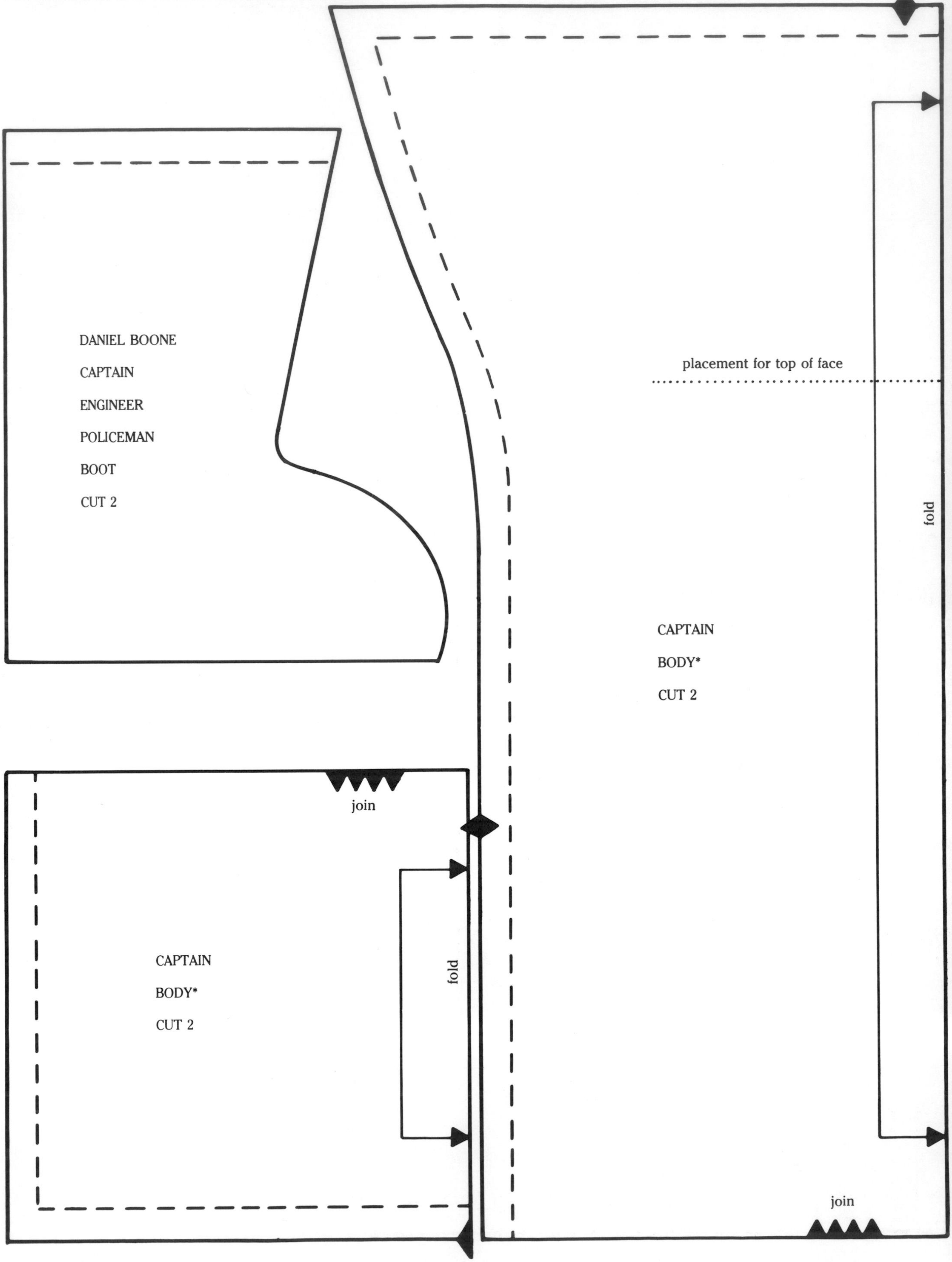

DANIEL BOONE

CAPTAIN

ENGINEER

POLICEMAN

BOOT

CUT 2

placement for top of face

fold

CAPTAIN

BODY*

CUT 2

join

CAPTAIN

BODY*

CUT 2

fold

join

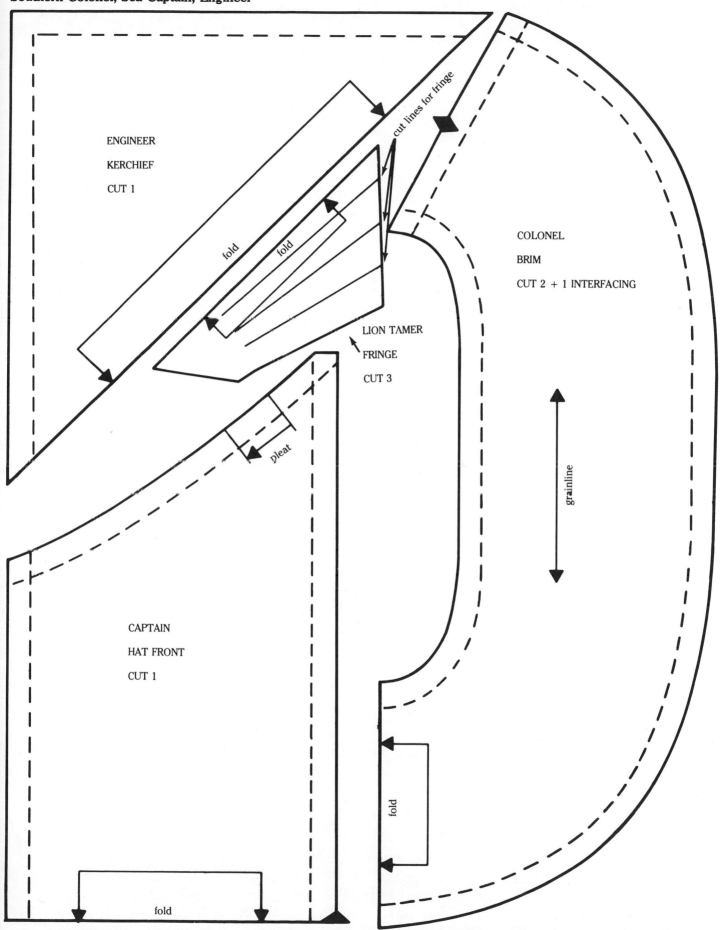

ENGINEER
KERCHIEF
CUT 1

fold

fold

cut lines for fringe

COLONEL
BRIM
CUT 2 + 1 INTERFACING

LION TAMER
FRINGE
CUT 3

grainline

pleat

CAPTAIN
HAT FRONT
CUT 1

fold

fold

fold

Daniel Boone, Southern Colonel, Sea Captain,
Engineer, Policeman, Lion Tamer

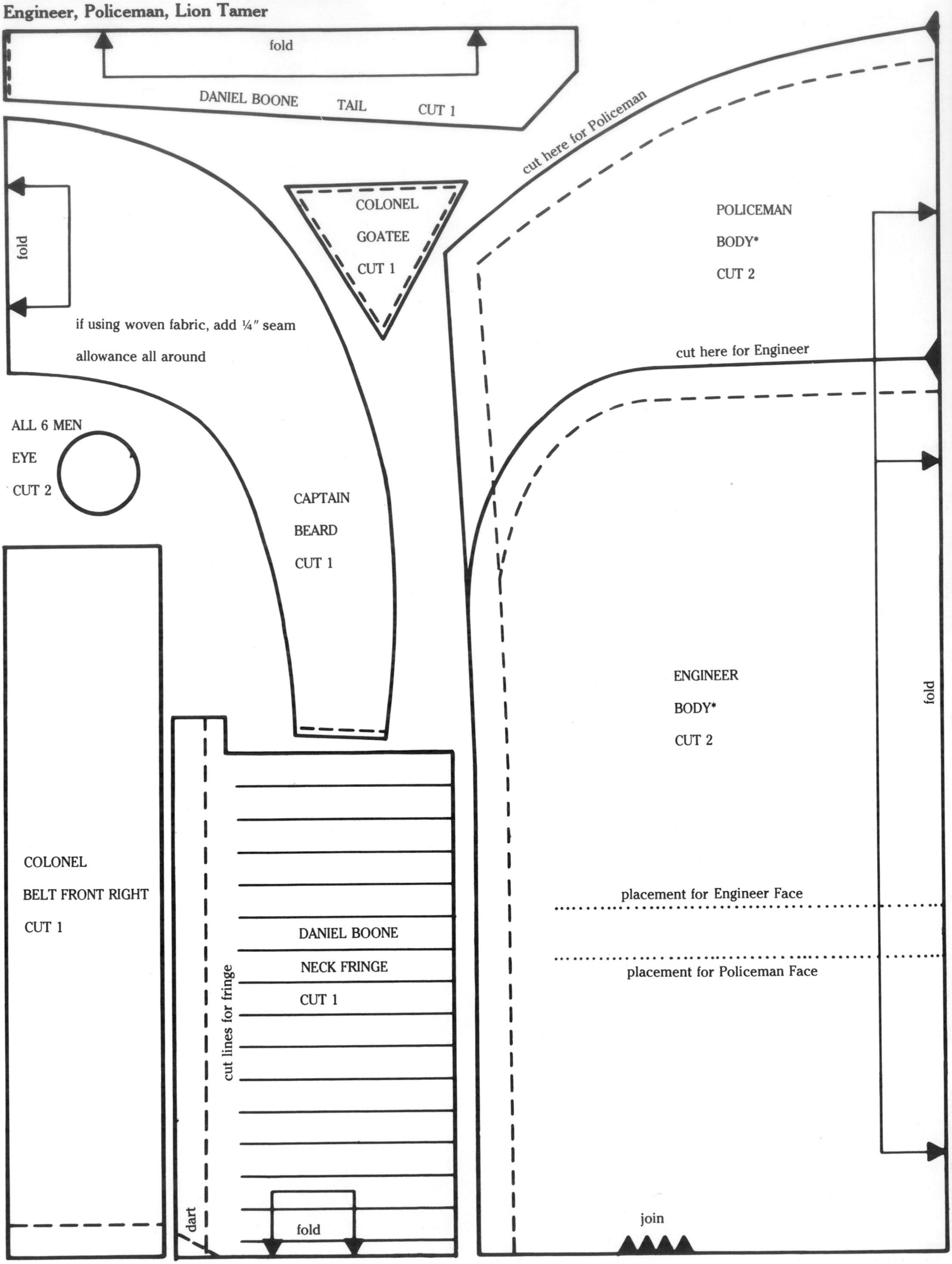

fold

DANIEL BOONE   TAIL   CUT 1

cut here for Policeman

COLONEL

GOATEE

CUT 1

fold

POLICEMAN

BODY*

CUT 2

if using woven fabric, add ¼" seam

allowance all around

cut here for Engineer

ALL 6 MEN

EYE

CUT 2

CAPTAIN

BEARD

CUT 1

ENGINEER

BODY*

CUT 2

fold

COLONEL

BELT FRONT RIGHT

CUT 1

placement for Engineer Face

cut lines for fringe

DANIEL BOONE

NECK FRINGE

CUT 1

placement for Policeman Face

dart

fold

join

110

Daniel Boone, Southern Colonel, Engineer,
Policeman, Lion Tamer

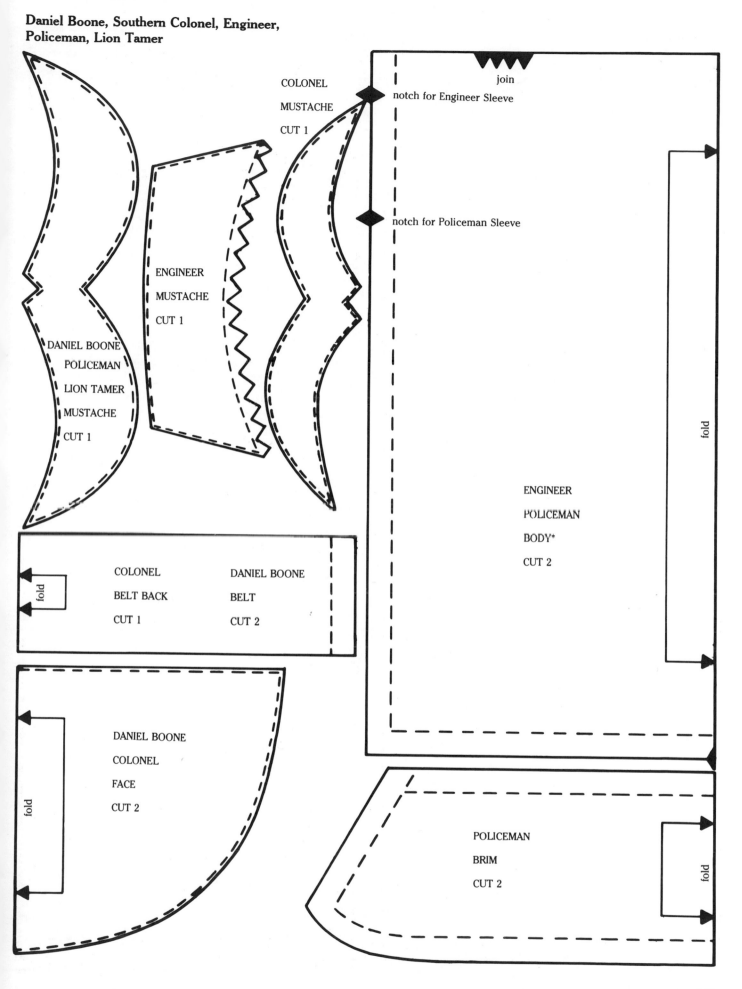

COLONEL
MUSTACHE
CUT 1

join

notch for Engineer Sleeve

notch for Policeman Sleeve

ENGINEER
MUSTACHE
CUT 1

DANIEL BOONE
POLICEMAN
LION TAMER
MUSTACHE
CUT 1

fold

ENGINEER
POLICEMAN
BODY*
CUT 2

fold

COLONEL
BELT BACK
CUT 1

DANIEL BOONE
BELT
CUT 2

fold

DANIEL BOONE
COLONEL
FACE
CUT 2

fold

POLICEMAN
BRIM
CUT 2

fold

111

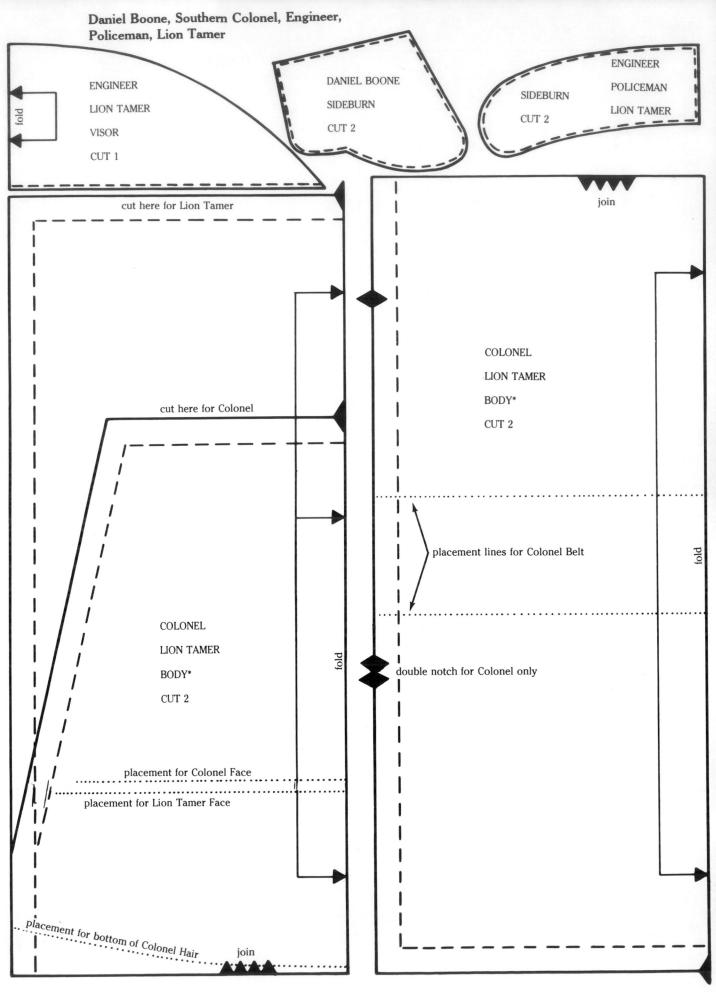

Daniel Boone, Southern Colonel, Engineer, Policeman, Lion Tamer

ENGINEER
LION TAMER
VISOR
CUT 1

fold

DANIEL BOONE
SIDEBURN
CUT 2

SIDEBURN
CUT 2

ENGINEER
POLICEMAN
LION TAMER

cut here for Lion Tamer

join

cut here for Colonel

COLONEL
LION TAMER
BODY*
CUT 2

placement lines for Colonel Belt

fold

fold

double notch for Colonel only

COLONEL
LION TAMER
BODY*
CUT 2

placement for Colonel Face

placement for Lion Tamer Face

placement for bottom of Colonel Hair

join

Miniature Sea Captain, Fisherman, and Union and Confederate Soldiers

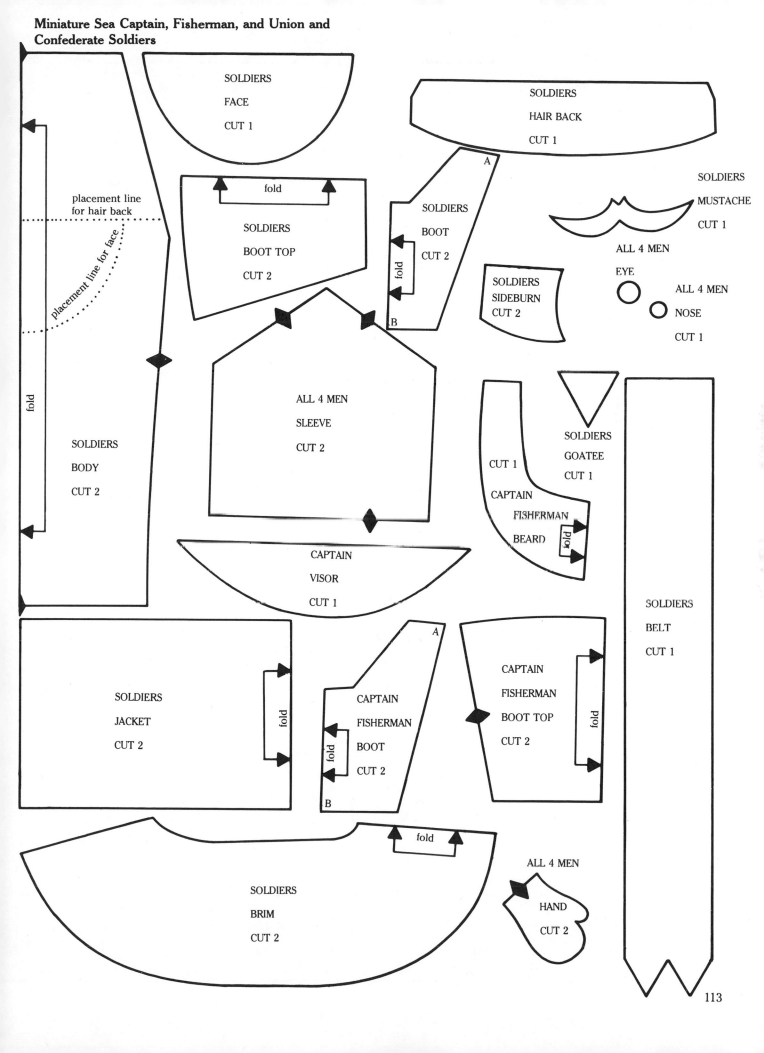

SOLDIERS
FACE
CUT 1

SOLDIERS
HAIR BACK
CUT 1

SOLDIERS
MUSTACHE
CUT 1
ALL 4 MEN

placement line
for hair back

placement line for face

fold

SOLDIERS
BOOT TOP
CUT 2

SOLDIERS
BOOT
CUT 2

fold

A

B

SOLDIERS
SIDEBURN
CUT 2

EYE
ALL 4 MEN

ALL 4 MEN
NOSE
CUT 1

SOLDIERS
BODY
CUT 2

fold

ALL 4 MEN
SLEEVE
CUT 2

CUT 1
CAPTAIN
FISHERMAN
BEARD

fold

SOLDIERS
GOATEE
CUT 1

CAPTAIN
VISOR
CUT 1

SOLDIERS
BELT
CUT 1

SOLDIERS
JACKET
CUT 2

fold

A

CAPTAIN
FISHERMAN
BOOT
CUT 2

fold

B

CAPTAIN
FISHERMAN
BOOT TOP
CUT 2

fold

fold

SOLDIERS
BRIM
CUT 2

ALL 4 MEN
HAND
CUT 2

113

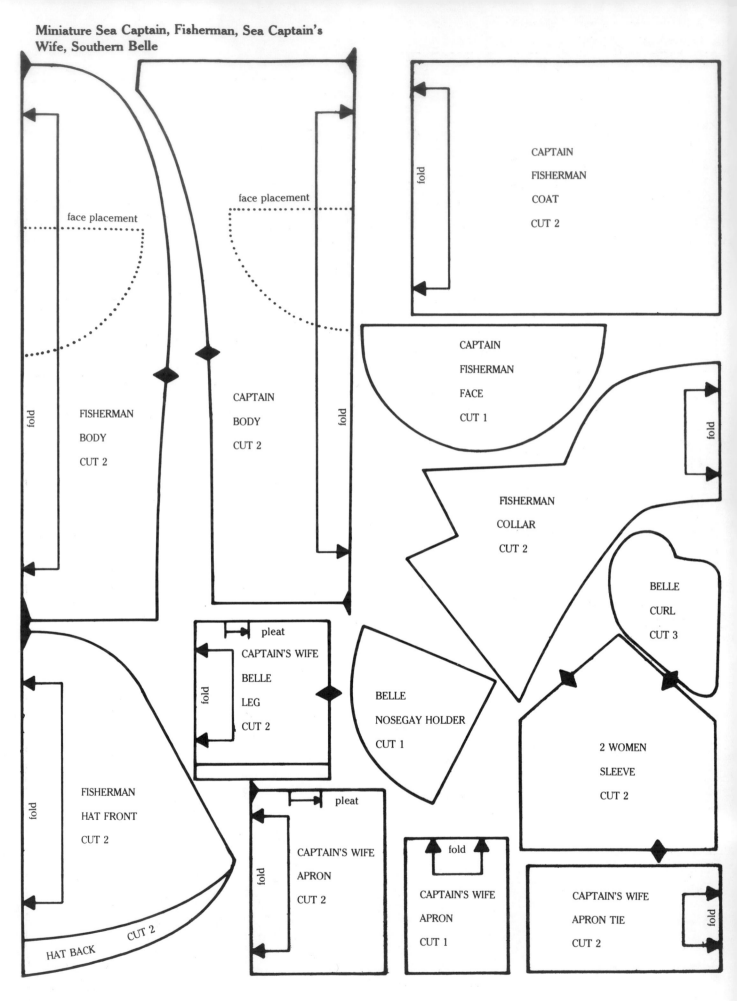

Miniature Sea Captain, Fisherman, Sea Captain's Wife, Southern Belle

face placement

face placement

fold

CAPTAIN
FISHERMAN
COAT
CUT 2

FISHERMAN
BODY
CUT 2

fold

CAPTAIN
BODY
CUT 2

fold

CAPTAIN
FISHERMAN
FACE
CUT 1

fold

FISHERMAN
COLLAR
CUT 2

BELLE
CURL
CUT 3

pleat

CAPTAIN'S WIFE
BELLE
LEG
CUT 2

fold

BELLE
NOSEGAY HOLDER
CUT 1

2 WOMEN
SLEEVE
CUT 2

FISHERMAN
HAT FRONT
CUT 2

fold

pleat

CAPTAIN'S WIFE
APRON
CUT 2

fold

fold

CAPTAIN'S WIFE
APRON
CUT 1

CAPTAIN'S WIFE
APRON TIE
CUT 2

fold

HAT BACK   CUT 2

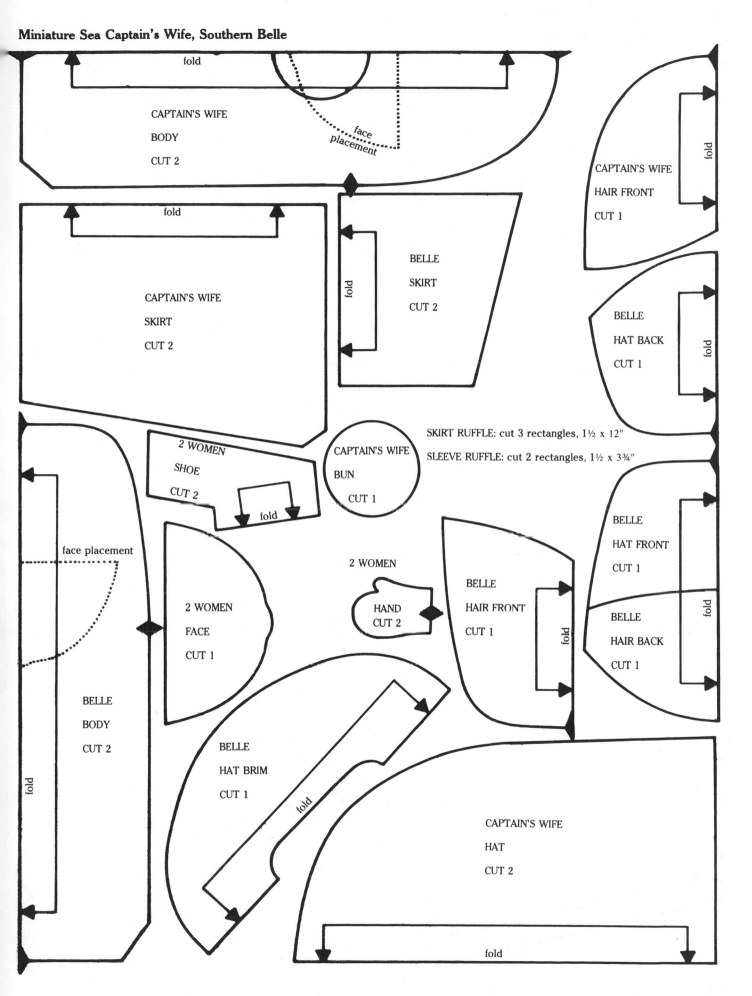

CAPTAIN'S WIFE
BODY
CUT 2

face placement

fold

CAPTAIN'S WIFE
HAIR FRONT
CUT 1

CAPTAIN'S WIFE
SKIRT
CUT 2

BELLE
SKIRT
CUT 2

fold

BELLE
HAT BACK
CUT 1

2 WOMEN
SHOE
CUT 2

CAPTAIN'S WIFE
BUN
CUT 1

SKIRT RUFFLE: cut 3 rectangles, 1½ x 12″

SLEEVE RUFFLE: cut 2 rectangles, 1½ x 3¾″

fold

face placement

2 WOMEN
FACE
CUT 1

2 WOMEN

HAND
CUT 2

BELLE
HAIR FRONT
CUT 1

BELLE
HAT FRONT
CUT 1

BELLE
HAIR BACK
CUT 1

BELLE
BODY
CUT 2

BELLE
HAT BRIM
CUT 1

fold

CAPTAIN'S WIFE
HAT
CUT 2

fold

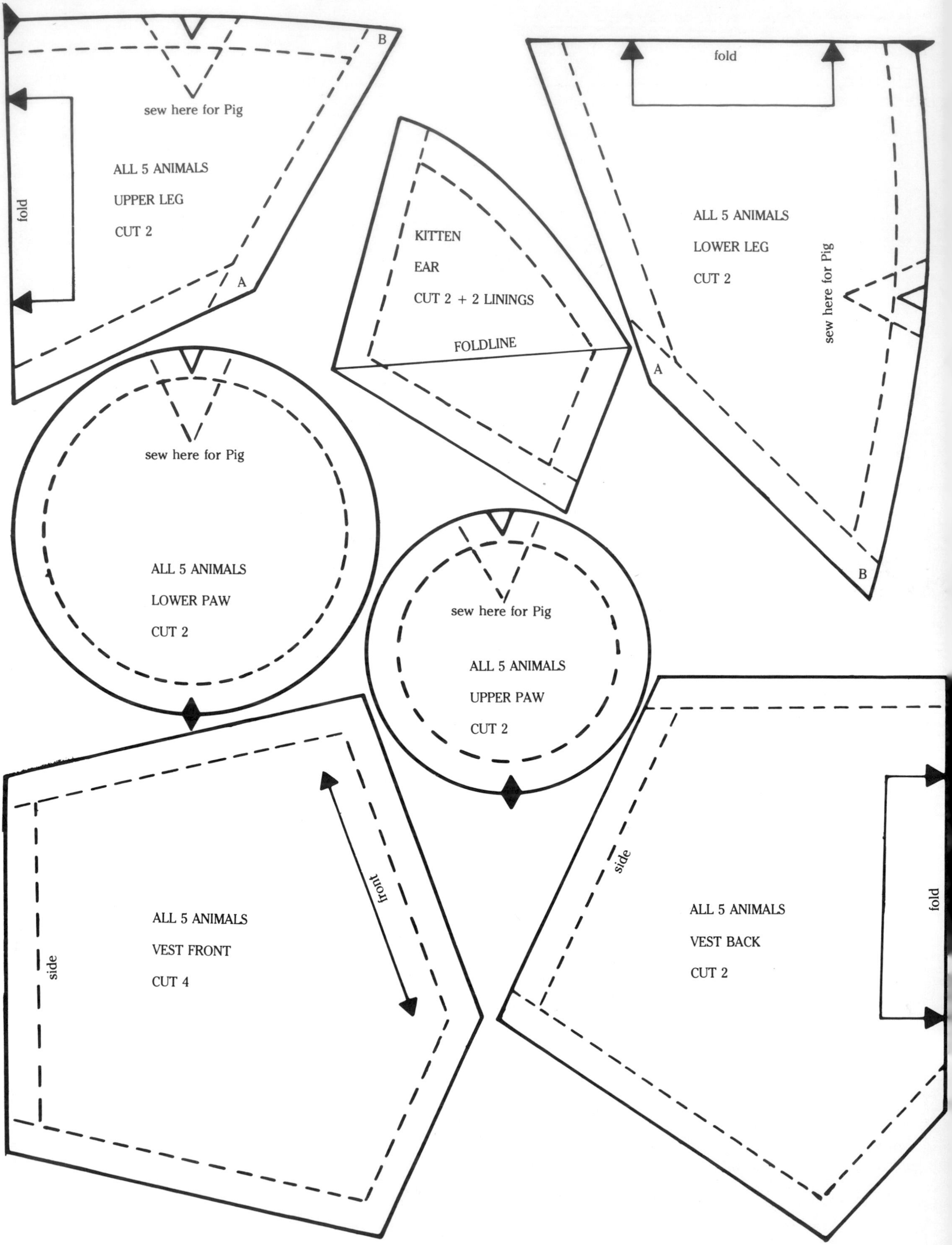

Bear, Rabbit, Panda, Pig, Kitten

sew here for Pig

ALL 5 ANIMALS
UPPER LEG
CUT 2

fold

B

A

fold

KITTEN
EAR
CUT 2 + 2 LININGS
FOLDLINE

ALL 5 ANIMALS
LOWER LEG
CUT 2

sew here for Pig

A

B

sew here for Pig

ALL 5 ANIMALS
LOWER PAW
CUT 2

sew here for Pig

ALL 5 ANIMALS
UPPER PAW
CUT 2

side

front

ALL 5 ANIMALS
VEST FRONT
CUT 4

side

ALL 5 ANIMALS
VEST BACK
CUT 2

fold

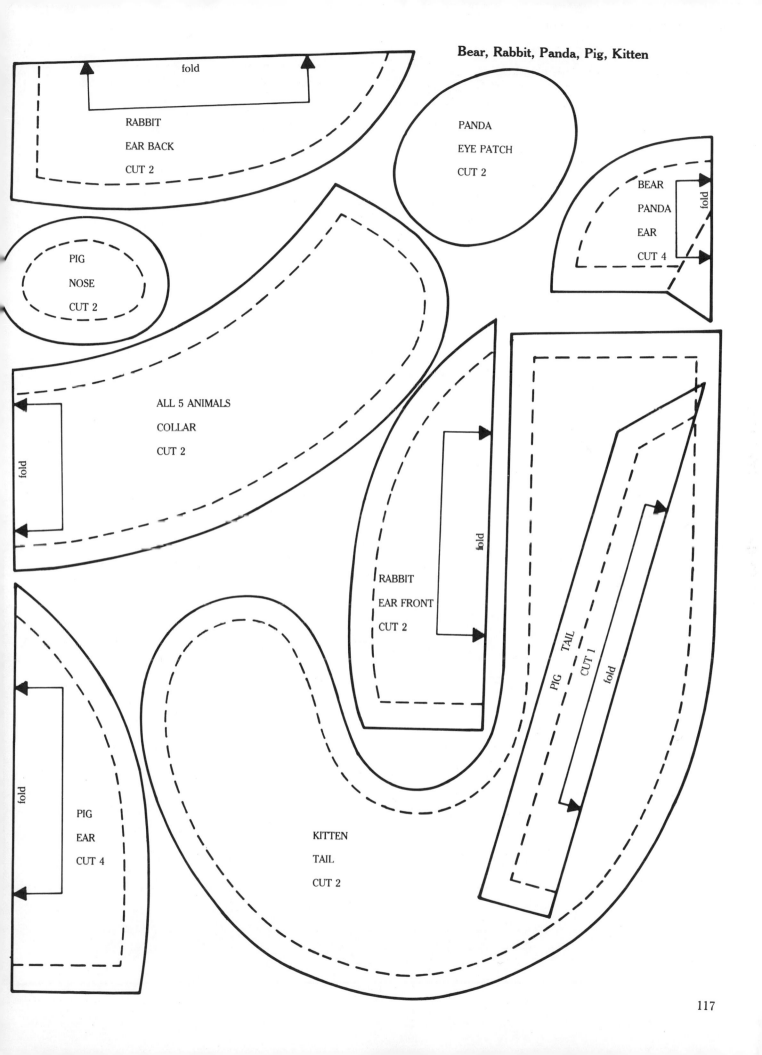

Bear, Rabbit, Panda, Pig, Kitten

fold

RABBIT
EAR BACK
CUT 2

PANDA
EYE PATCH
CUT 2

BEAR
PANDA
EAR
CUT 4

fold

PIG
NOSE
CUT 2

ALL 5 ANIMALS
COLLAR
CUT 2

fold

RABBIT
EAR FRONT
CUT 2

fold

PIG   TAIL
CUT 1
fold

PIG
EAR
CUT 4

fold

KITTEN
TAIL
CUT 2

117

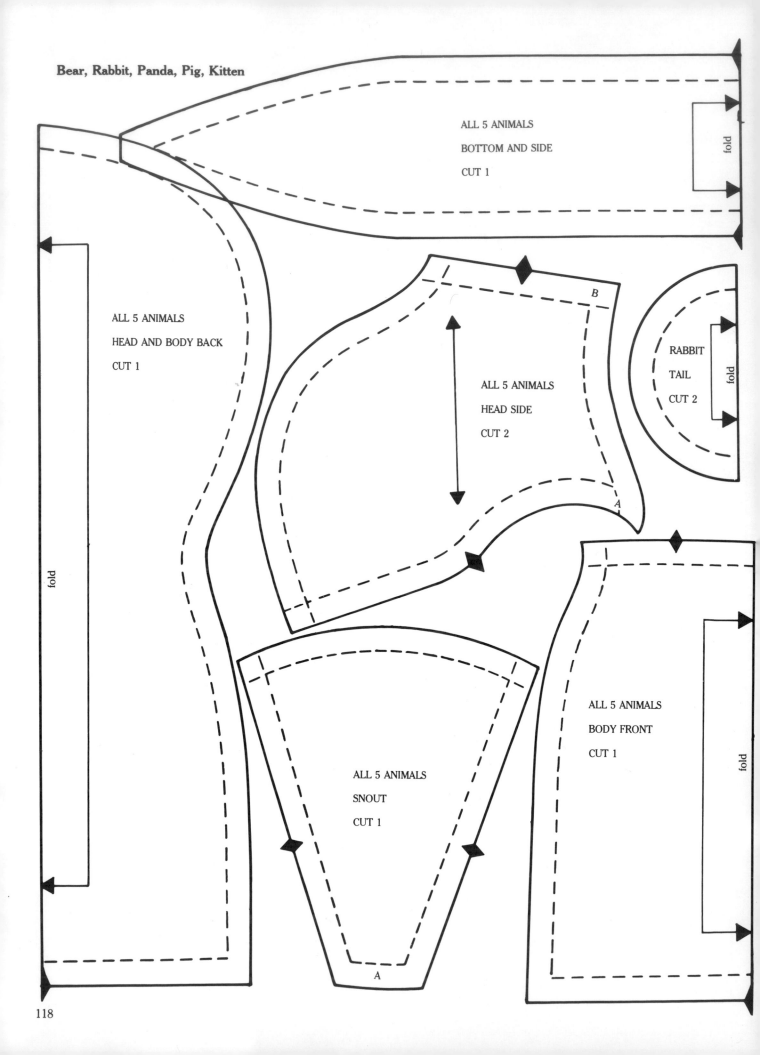

Bear, Rabbit, Panda, Pig, Kitten

ALL 5 ANIMALS
BOTTOM AND SIDE
CUT 1

fold

ALL 5 ANIMALS
HEAD AND BODY BACK
CUT 1

B

ALL 5 ANIMALS
HEAD SIDE
CUT 2

RABBIT
TAIL
CUT 2

fold

A

fold

ALL 5 ANIMALS
BODY FRONT
CUT 1

ALL 5 ANIMALS
SNOUT
CUT 1

fold

A

Lion, Tiger

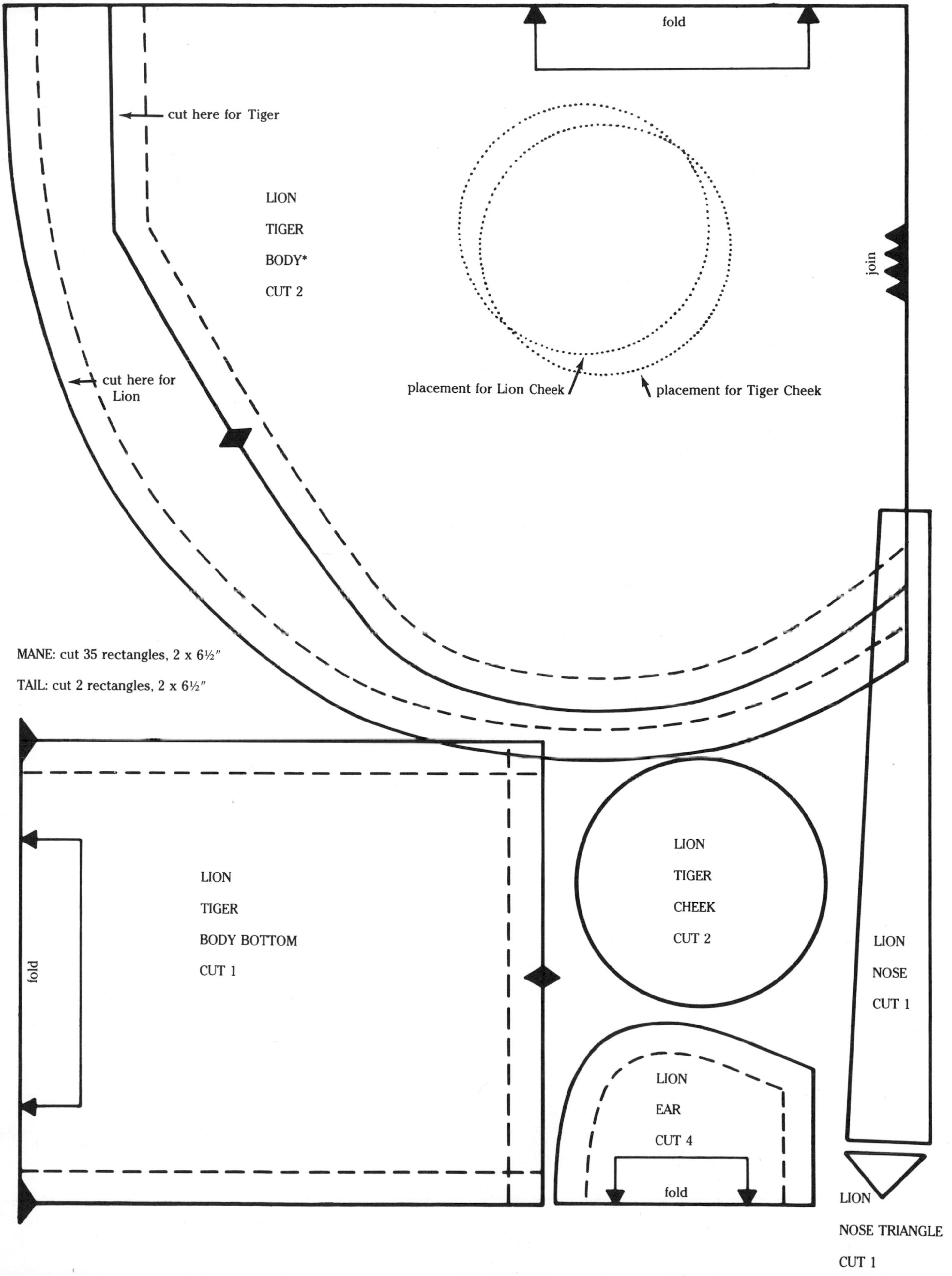

fold

cut here for Tiger

LION

TIGER

BODY*

CUT 2

join

cut here for
Lion

placement for Lion Cheek   placement for Tiger Cheek

MANE: cut 35 rectangles, 2 x 6½"

TAIL: cut 2 rectangles, 2 x 6½"

LION

TIGER

BODY BOTTOM

CUT 1

fold

LION

TIGER

CHEEK

CUT 2

LION

NOSE

CUT 1

LION

EAR

CUT 4

fold

LION

NOSE TRIANGLE

CUT 1

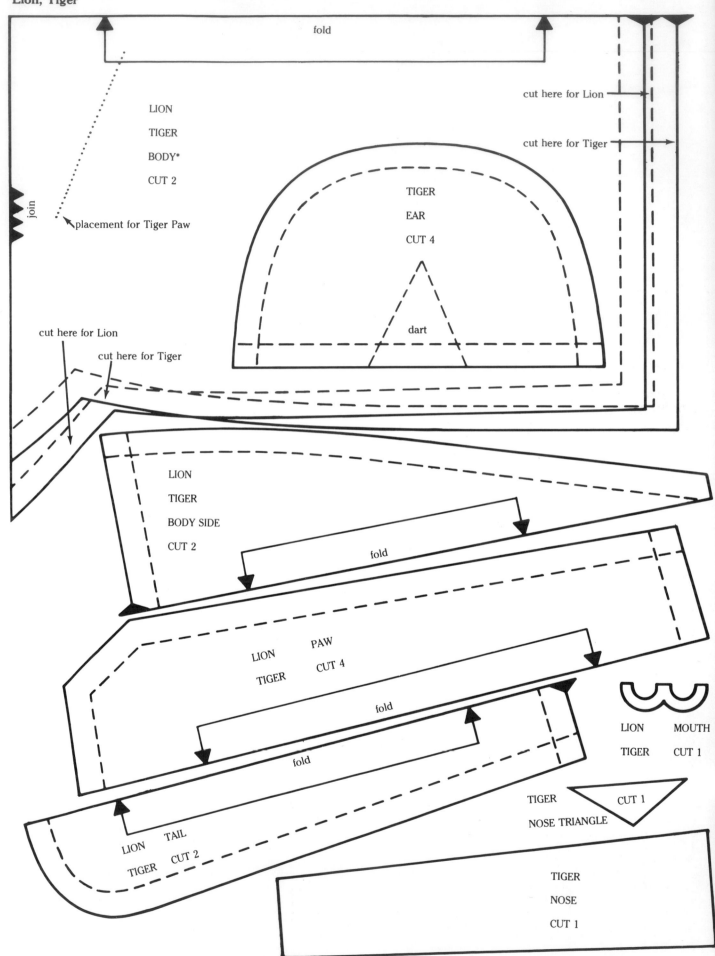

Lion, Tiger

fold

cut here for Lion

cut here for Tiger

join

placement for Tiger Paw

LION
TIGER
BODY*
CUT 2

TIGER
EAR
CUT 4

dart

cut here for Lion

cut here for Tiger

LION
TIGER
BODY SIDE
CUT 2

fold

LION   PAW
TIGER   CUT 4

fold

LION   MOUTH
TIGER   CUT 1

fold

fold

TIGER
NOSE TRIANGLE

CUT 1

LION   TAIL
TIGER   CUT 2

TIGER
NOSE
CUT 1

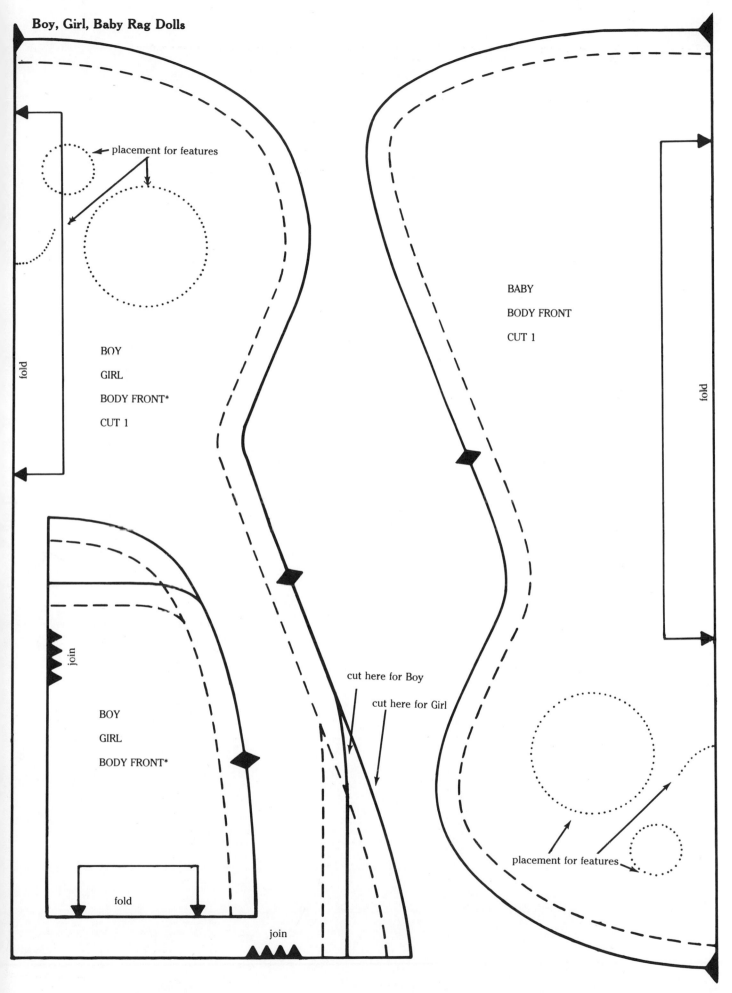

placement for features

BOY
GIRL
BODY FRONT*
CUT 1

fold

BABY
BODY FRONT
CUT 1

fold

join

BOY
GIRL
BODY FRONT*

cut here for Boy

cut here for Girl

fold

join

placement for features

121

Boy, Girl Rag Doll

GIRL

DRESS: cut 2 rectangles, 11 x 18″

PANTIES: cut 2 rectangles, 6 x 12″

BOW: cut 1 rectangle, 3 x 22″

KNOT: cut 1 square, 3 x 3″

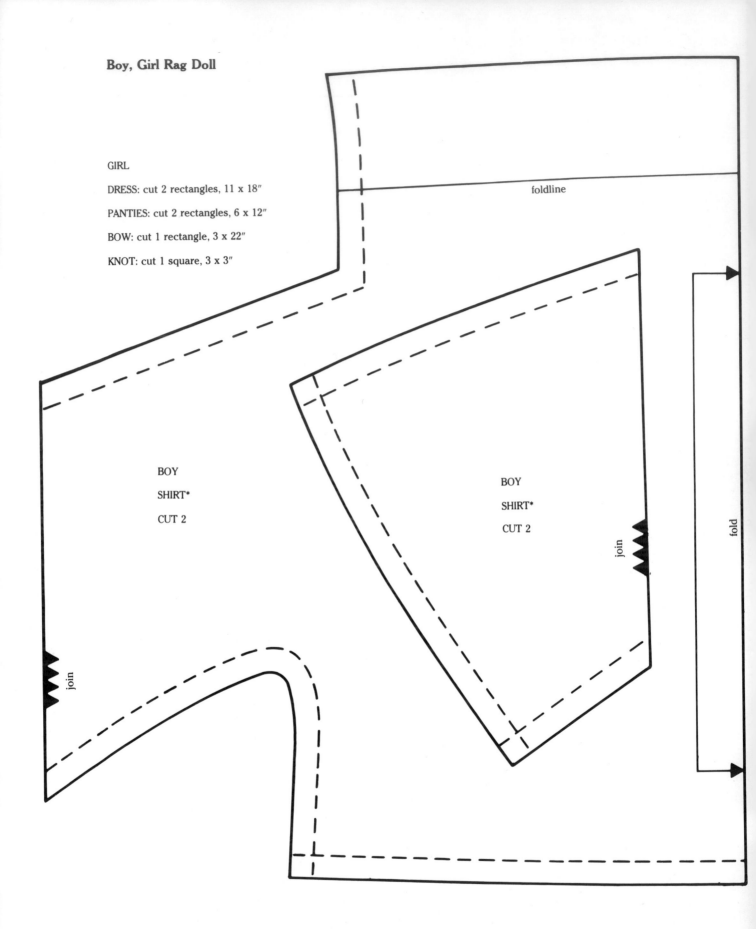

foldline

BOY
SHIRT*
CUT 2

BOY
SHIRT*
CUT 2

join

join

fold

Boy, Girl, Baby Rag Doll

Note: Shoe sole pattern is same as foot sole pattern

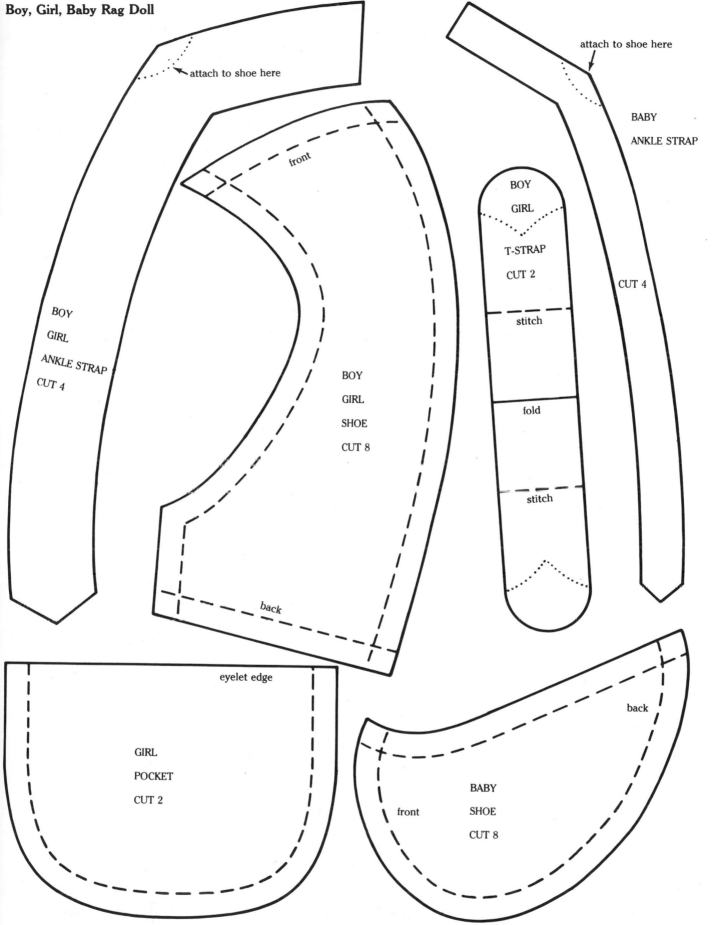

attach to shoe here

attach to shoe here

BABY

ANKLE STRAP

front

BOY

GIRL

T-STRAP

CUT 2

stitch

fold

stitch

CUT 4

BOY

GIRL

ANKLE STRAP

CUT 4

BOY

GIRL

SHOE

CUT 8

back

eyelet edge

GIRL

POCKET

CUT 2

back

BABY

SHOE

CUT 8

front

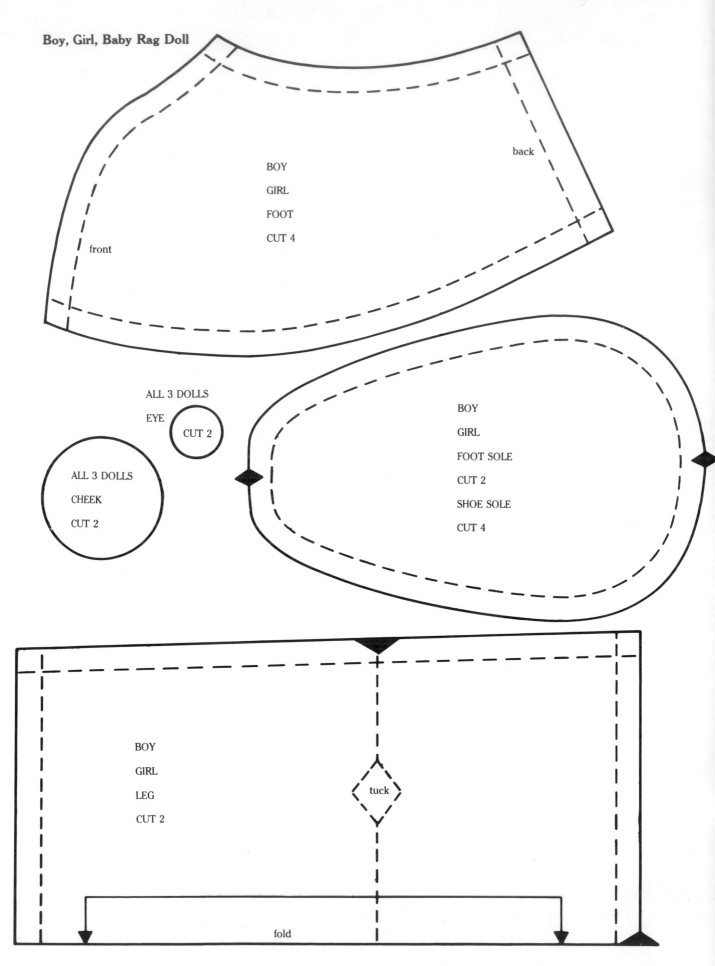

Boy, Girl, Baby Rag Doll

back

BOY
GIRL
FOOT
CUT 4

front

ALL 3 DOLLS
EYE
CUT 2

BOY
GIRL
FOOT SOLE
CUT 2
SHOE SOLE
CUT 4

ALL 3 DOLLS
CHEEK
CUT 2

BOY
GIRL
LEG
CUT 2

tuck

fold

124

Boy, Girl, Baby Rag Doll

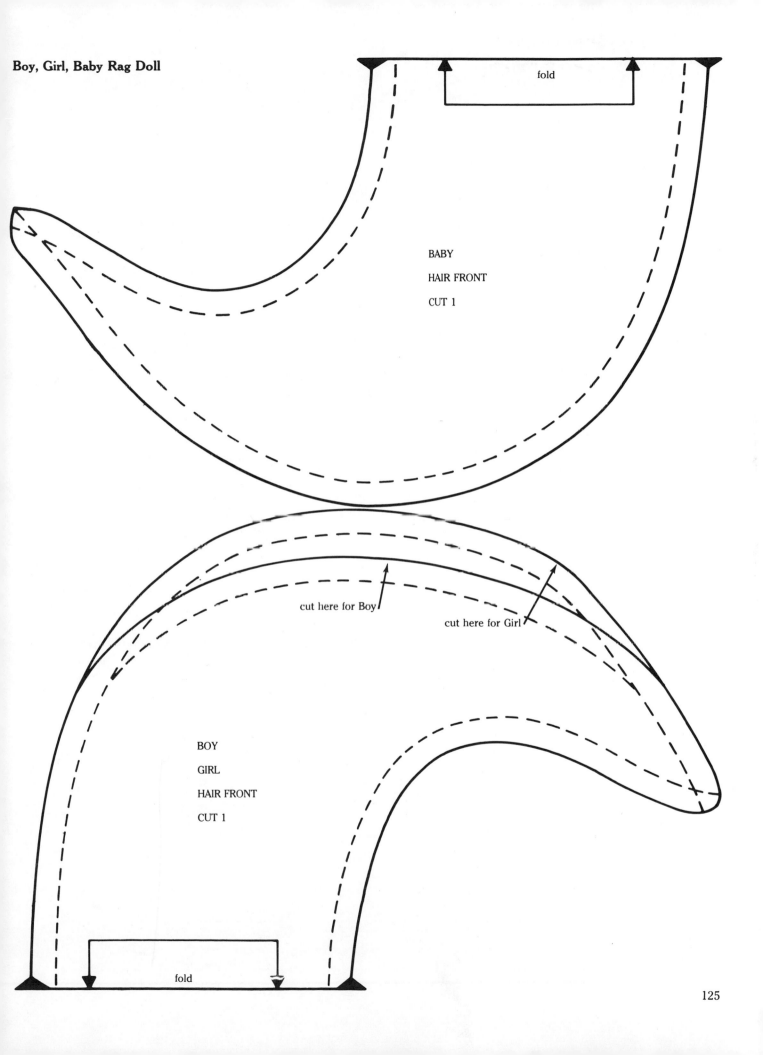

fold

BABY

HAIR FRONT

CUT 1

cut here for Boy

cut here for Girl

BOY

GIRL

HAIR FRONT

CUT 1

fold

Boy, Girl, Baby Rag Doll

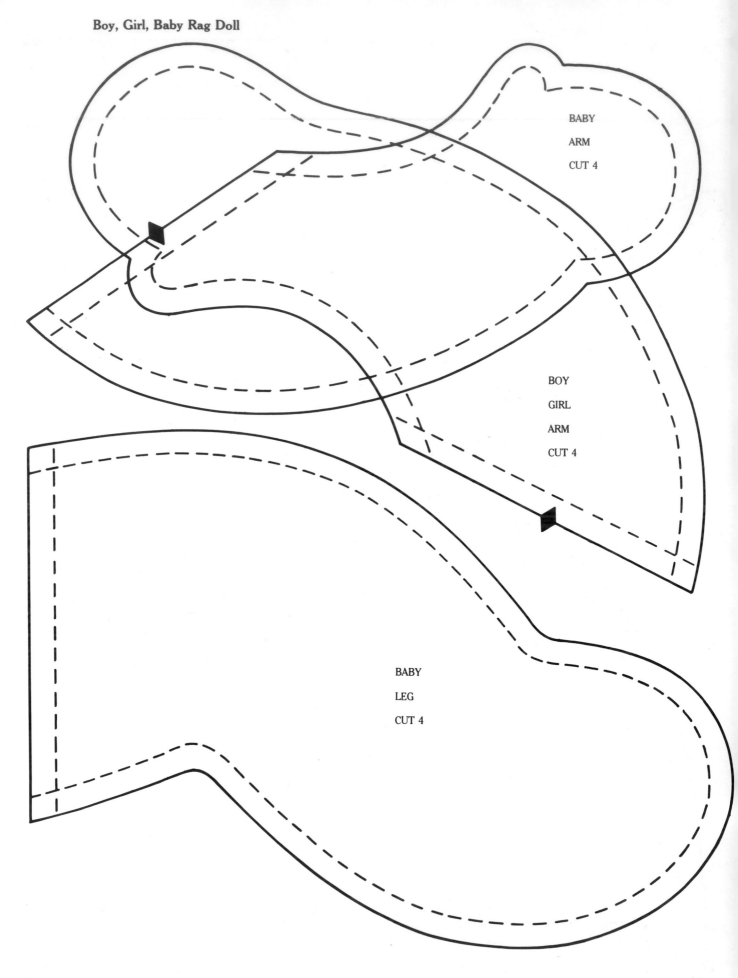

BABY
ARM
CUT 4

BOY
GIRL
ARM
CUT 4

BABY
LEG
CUT 4

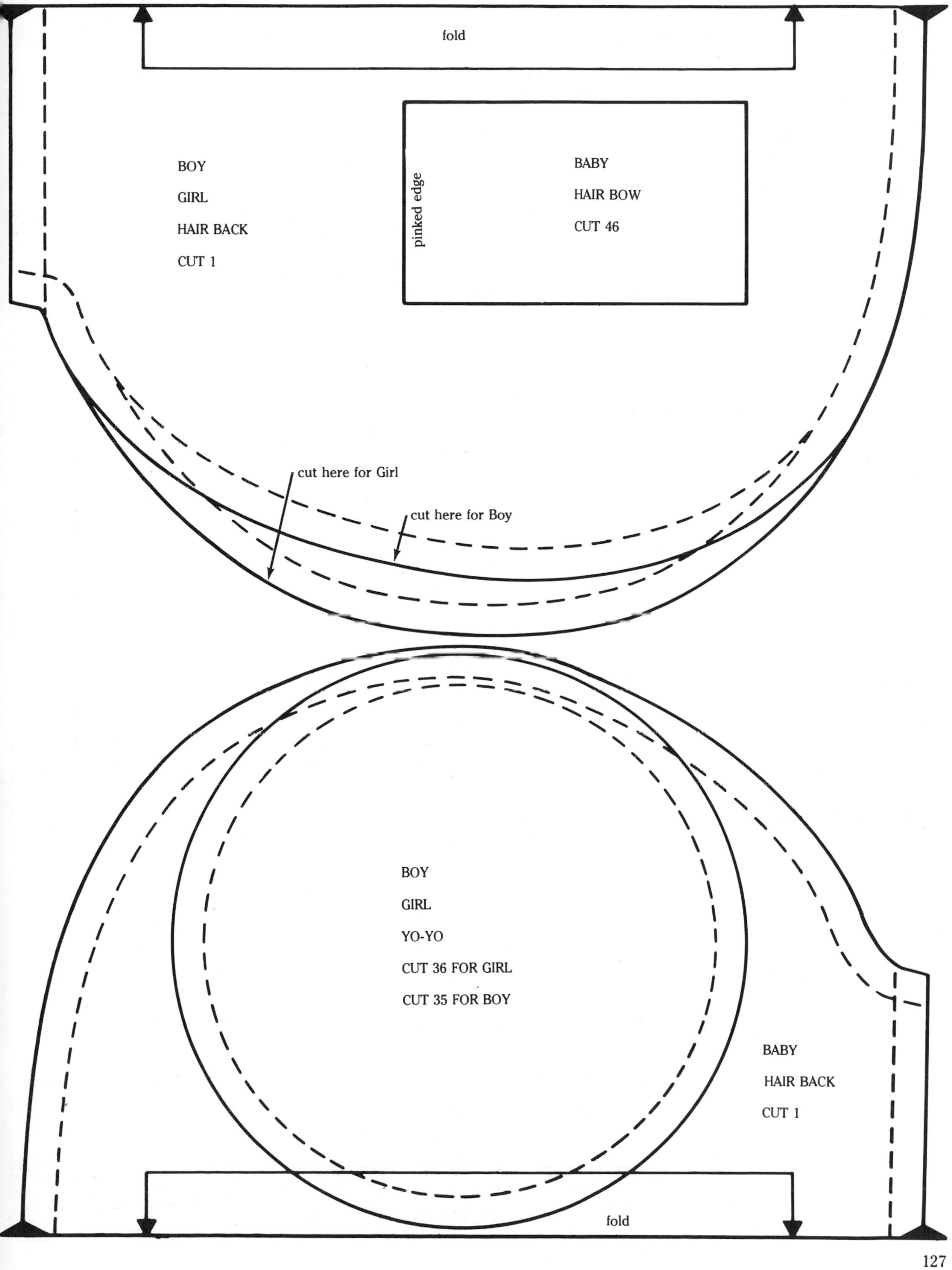

Boy, Girl, Baby Rag Doll

fold

BOY

GIRL

HAIR BACK

CUT 1

pinked edge

BABY

HAIR BOW

CUT 46

cut here for Girl

cut here for Boy

BOY

GIRL

YO-YO

CUT 36 FOR GIRL

CUT 35 FOR BOY

BABY

HAIR BACK

CUT 1

fold

127

Boy, Girl, Baby Rag Doll

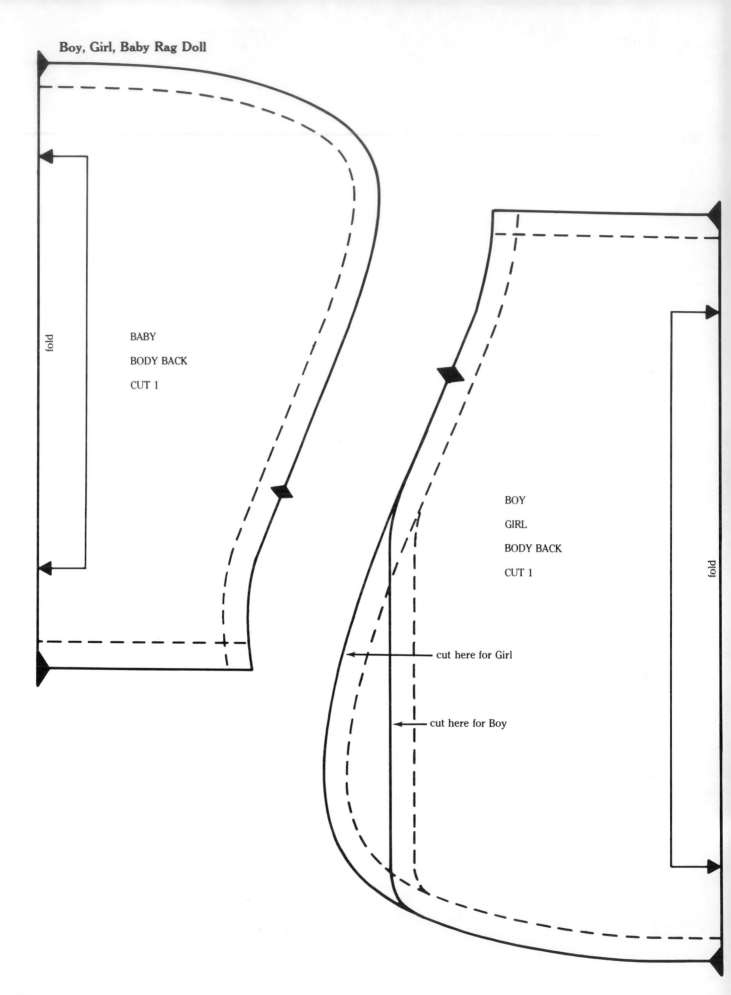

fold

BABY
BODY BACK
CUT 1

BOY
GIRL
BODY BACK
CUT 1

fold

cut here for Girl

cut here for Boy

Boy, Girl, Baby Rag Doll

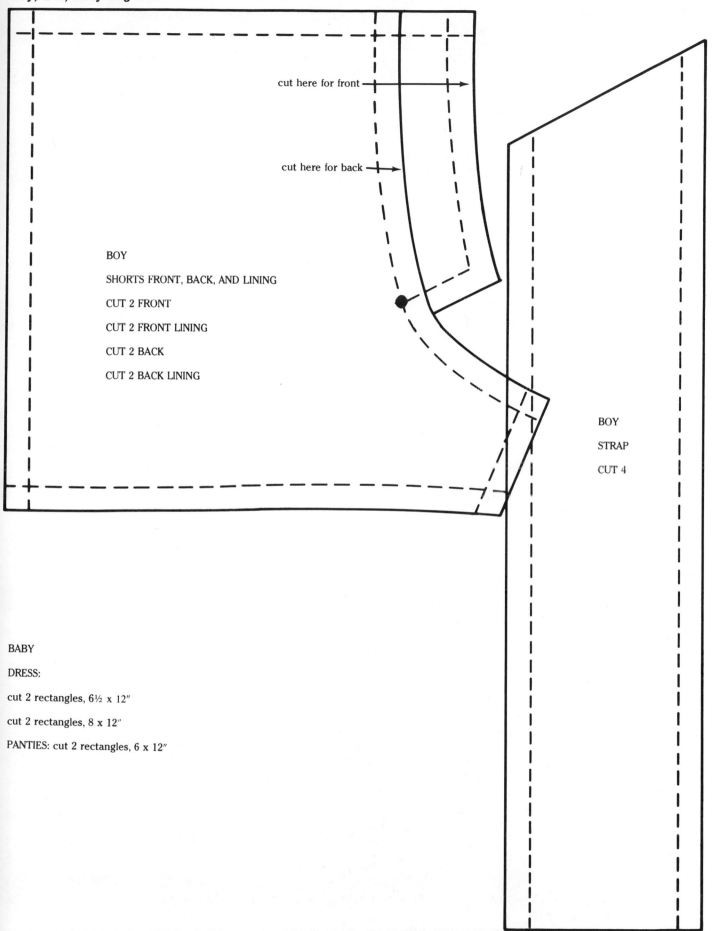

cut here for front

cut here for back

BOY

SHORTS FRONT, BACK, AND LINING

CUT 2 FRONT

CUT 2 FRONT LINING

CUT 2 BACK

CUT 2 BACK LINING

BOY

STRAP

CUT 4

BABY

DRESS:

cut 2 rectangles, 6½ x 12″

cut 2 rectangles, 8 x 12″

PANTIES: cut 2 rectangles, 6 x 12″

Cupid Pillow-Doll

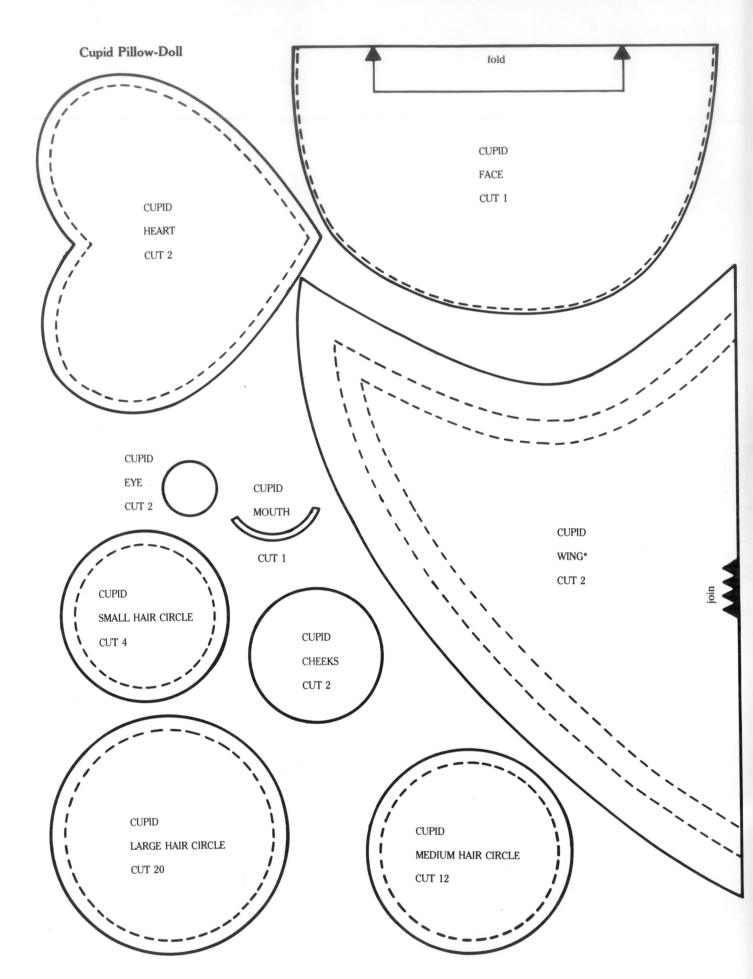

fold

CUPID
FACE
CUT 1

CUPID
HEART
CUT 2

CUPID
EYE
CUT 2

CUPID
MOUTH

CUT 1

CUPID
WING*
CUT 2

join

CUPID
SMALL HAIR CIRCLE
CUT 4

CUPID
CHEEKS
CUT 2

CUPID
LARGE HAIR CIRCLE
CUT 20

CUPID
MEDIUM HAIR CIRCLE
CUT 12

130

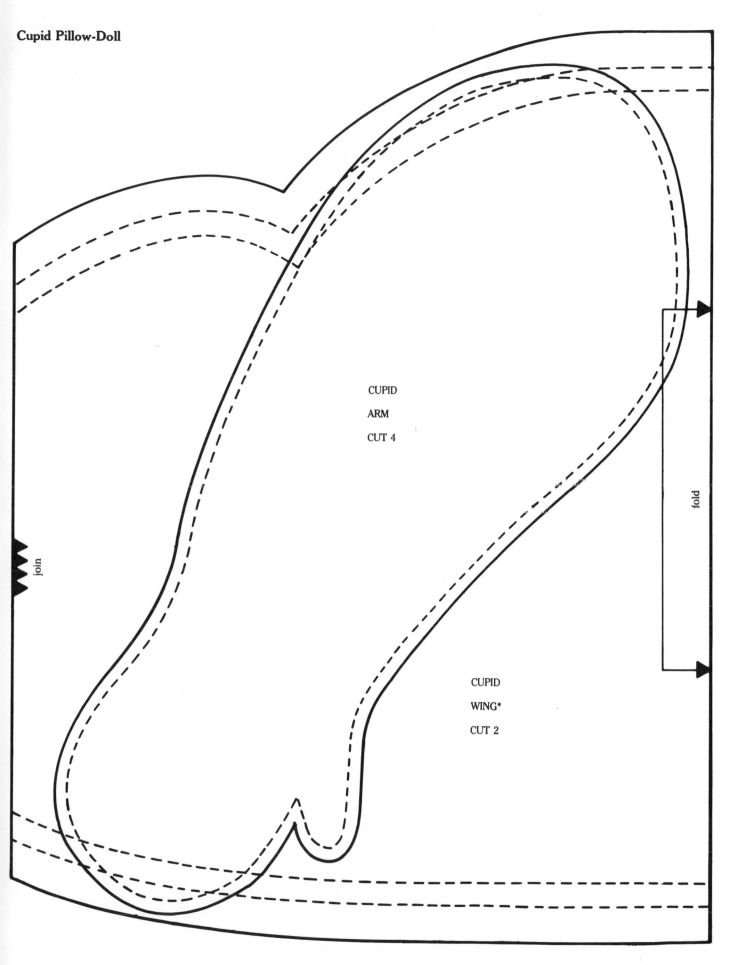

CUPID

ARM

CUT 4

CUPID

WING*

CUT 2

fold

join

Cupid Pillow-Doll

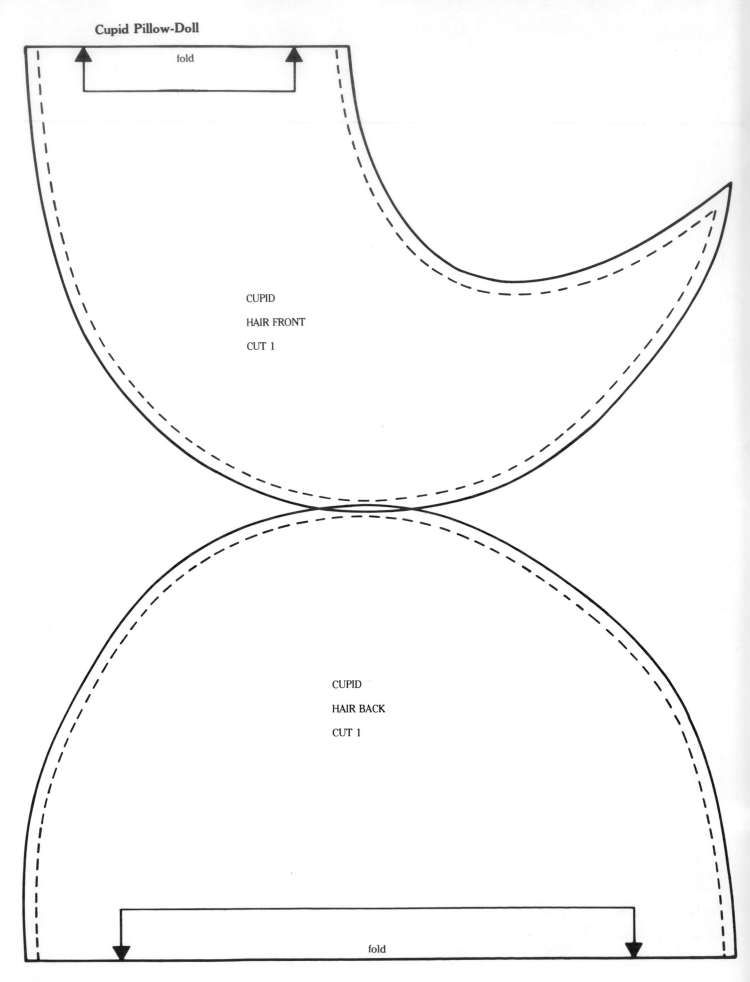

fold

CUPID

HAIR FRONT

CUT 1

CUPID

HAIR BACK

CUT 1

fold

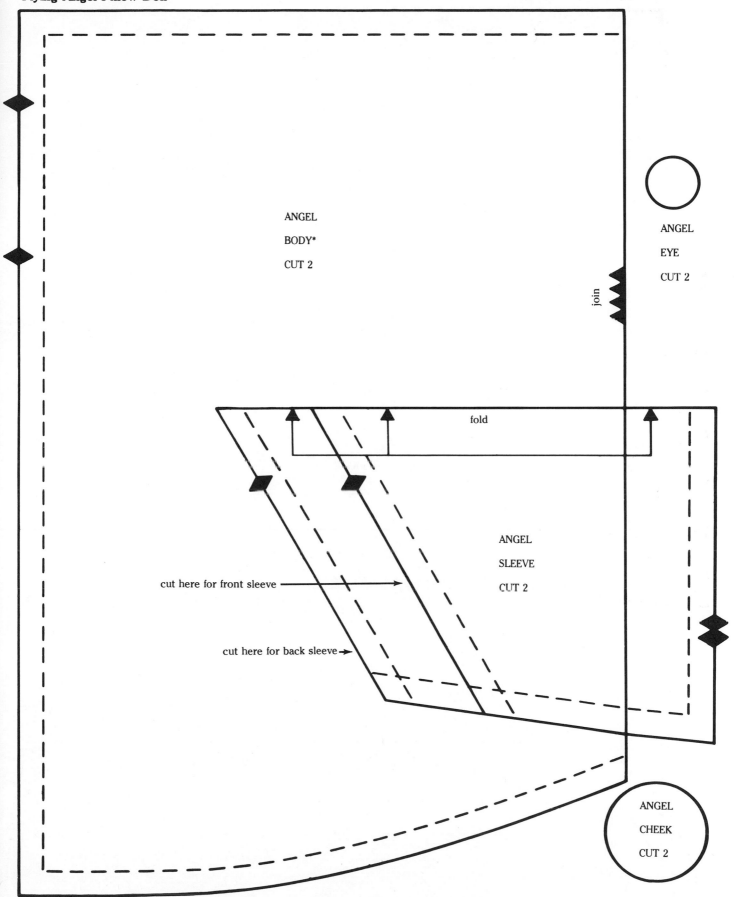

ANGEL

BODY*

CUT 2

ANGEL

EYE

CUT 2

join

fold

ANGEL

SLEEVE

CUT 2

cut here for front sleeve →

cut here for back sleeve →

ANGEL

CHEEK

CUT 2

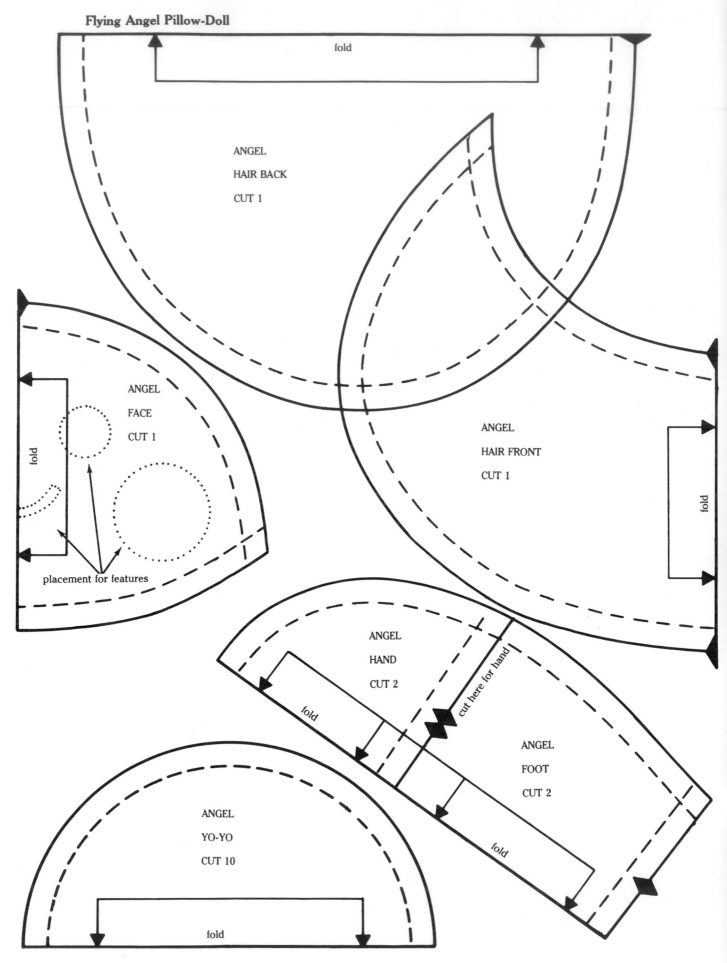

Flying Angel Pillow-Doll

fold

ANGEL
HAIR BACK
CUT 1

ANGEL
HAIR FRONT
CUT 1

fold

ANGEL
FACE
CUT 1

fold

placement for features

ANGEL
HAND
CUT 2

cut here for hand

fold

ANGEL
FOOT
CUT 2

fold

ANGEL
YO-YO
CUT 10

fold

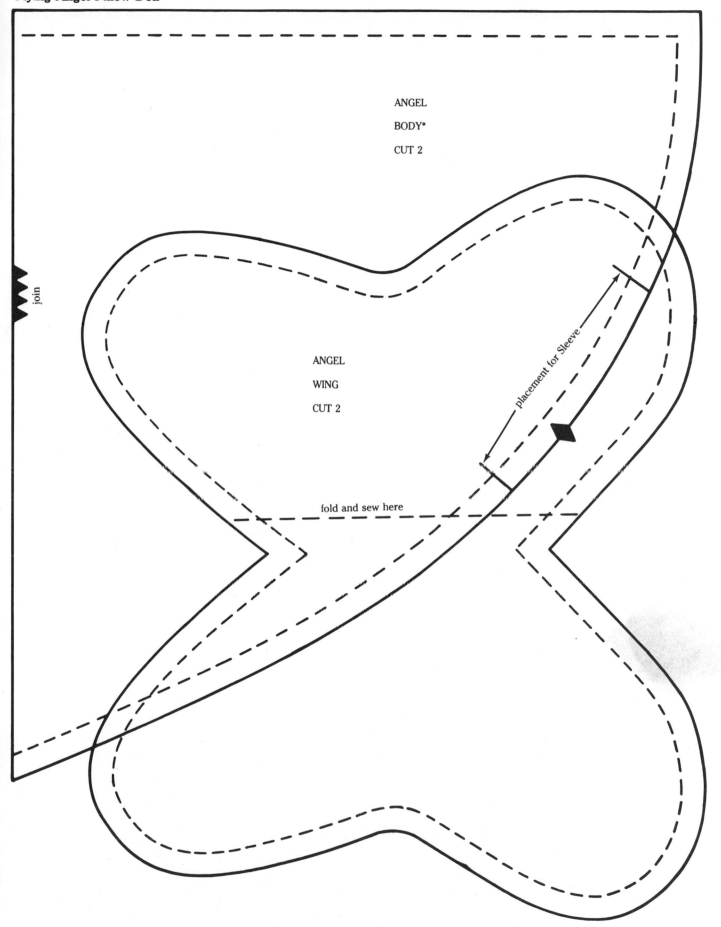

ANGEL
BODY*
CUT 2

ANGEL
WING
CUT 2

join

placement for Sleeve

fold and sew here

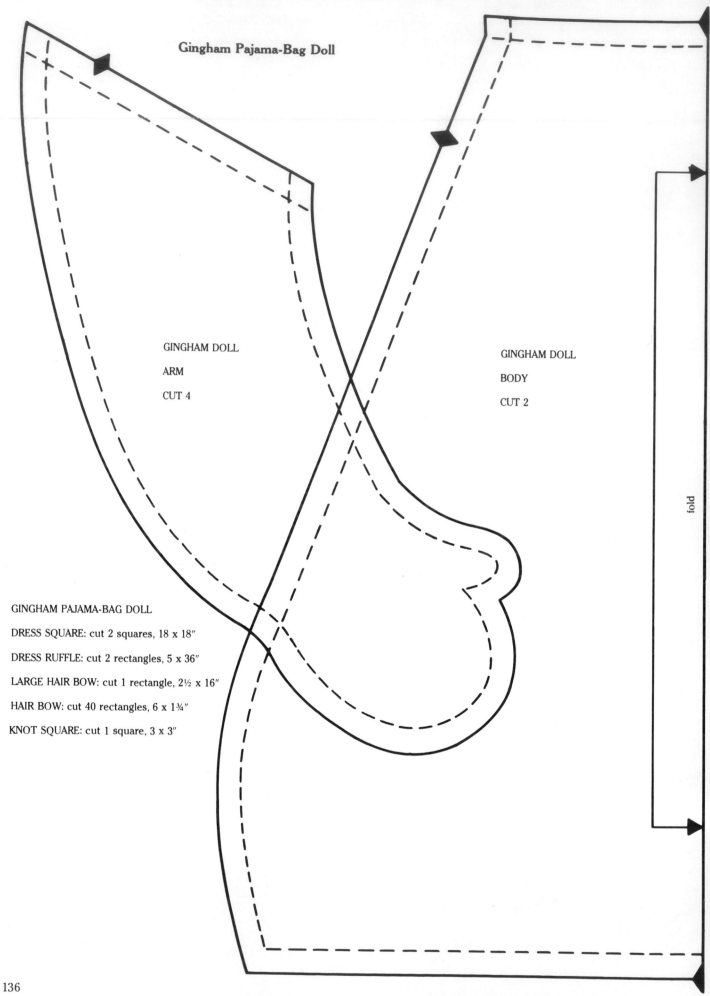

Gingham Pajama-Bag Doll

GINGHAM DOLL

ARM

CUT 4

GINGHAM DOLL

BODY

CUT 2

fold

GINGHAM PAJAMA-BAG DOLL

DRESS SQUARE: cut 2 squares, 18 x 18″

DRESS RUFFLE: cut 2 rectangles, 5 x 36″

LARGE HAIR BOW: cut 1 rectangle, 2½ x 16″

HAIR BOW: cut 40 rectangles, 6 x 1¾″

KNOT SQUARE: cut 1 square, 3 x 3″

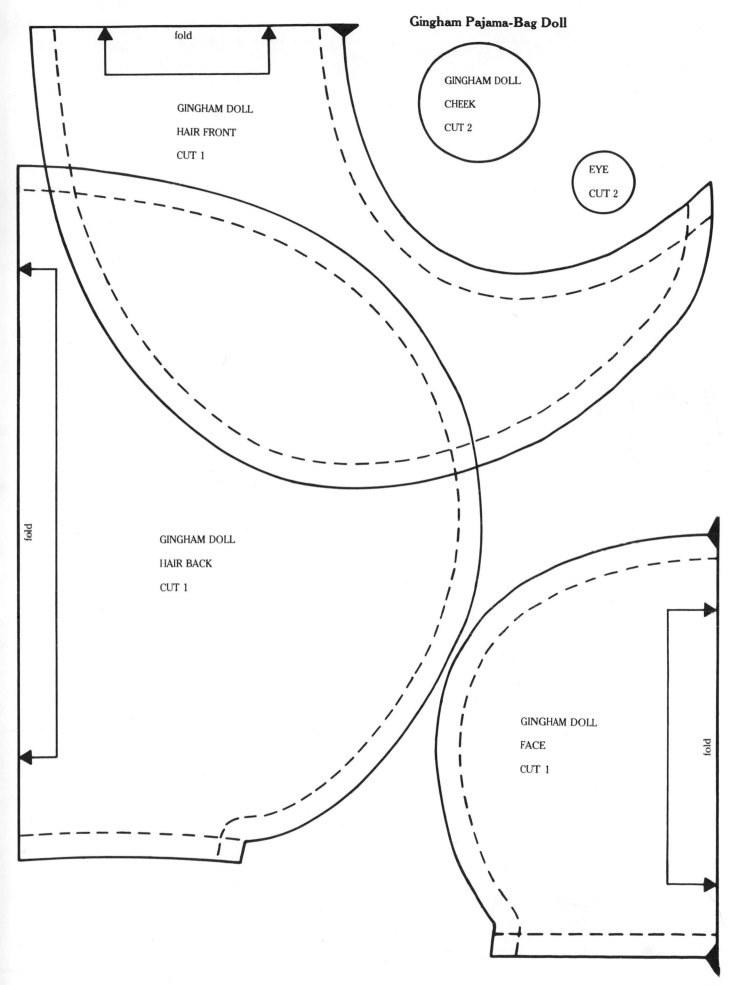

Gingham Pajama-Bag Doll

fold

GINGHAM DOLL
HAIR FRONT
CUT 1

GINGHAM DOLL
CHEEK
CUT 2

EYE
CUT 2

fold

GINGHAM DOLL
HAIR BACK
CUT 1

GINGHAM DOLL
FACE
CUT 1

fold

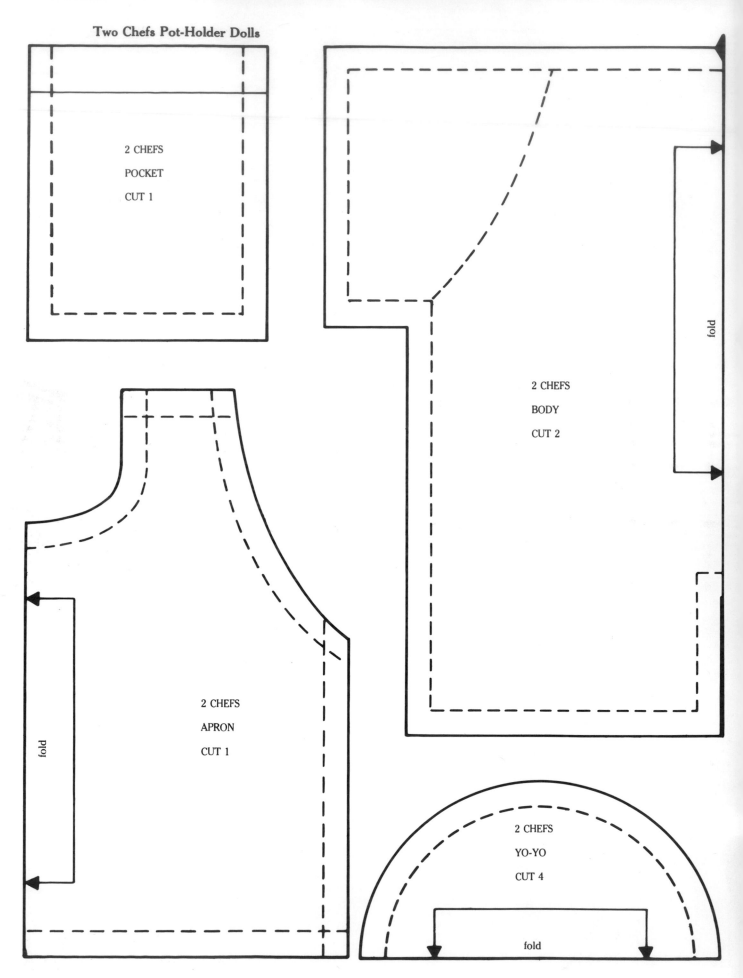

Two Chefs Pot-Holder Dolls

2 CHEFS
POCKET
CUT 1

2 CHEFS
BODY
CUT 2

fold

2 CHEFS
APRON
CUT 1

fold

2 CHEFS
YO-YO
CUT 4

fold

Two Chefs Pot-Holder Dolls

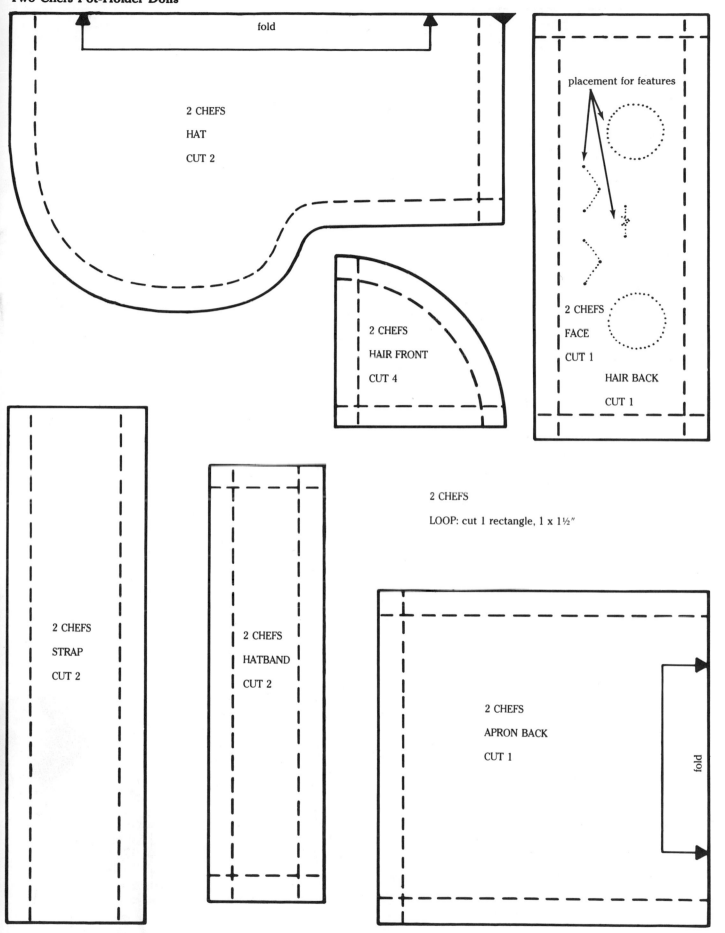

fold

2 CHEFS

HAT

CUT 2

placement for features

2 CHEFS

FACE

CUT 1

HAIR BACK

CUT 1

2 CHEFS

HAIR FRONT

CUT 4

2 CHEFS

LOOP: cut 1 rectangle, 1 x 1½″

2 CHEFS

STRAP

CUT 2

2 CHEFS

HATBAND

CUT 2

2 CHEFS

APRON BACK

CUT 1

fold

139

French Sailor Pillow-Doll

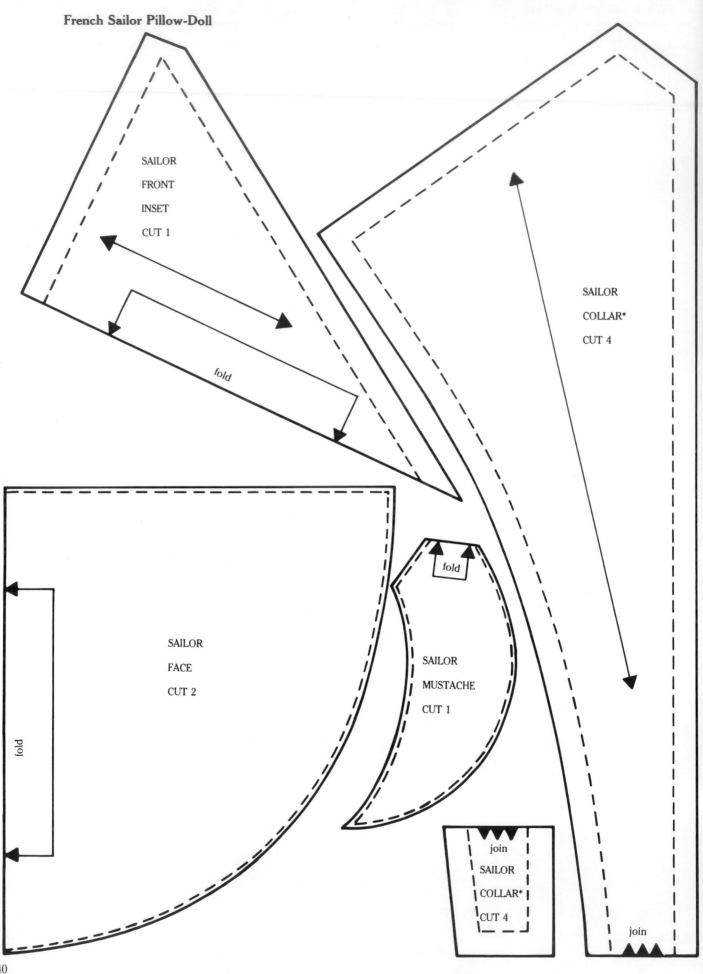

SAILOR
FRONT
INSET
CUT 1

fold

SAILOR
COLLAR*
CUT 4

fold

SAILOR
FACE
CUT 2

fold

SAILOR
MUSTACHE
CUT 1

join
SAILOR
COLLAR*
CUT 4

join

French Sailor Pillow-Doll

SAILOR
BODY*
CUT 2
placement lines
FACE
SIDEBURN
EYE
MUSTACHE
FRONT INSET
fold
join
SAILOR
POM-PON
CUT 1
fold
SAILOR
SIDEBURN
CUT 2

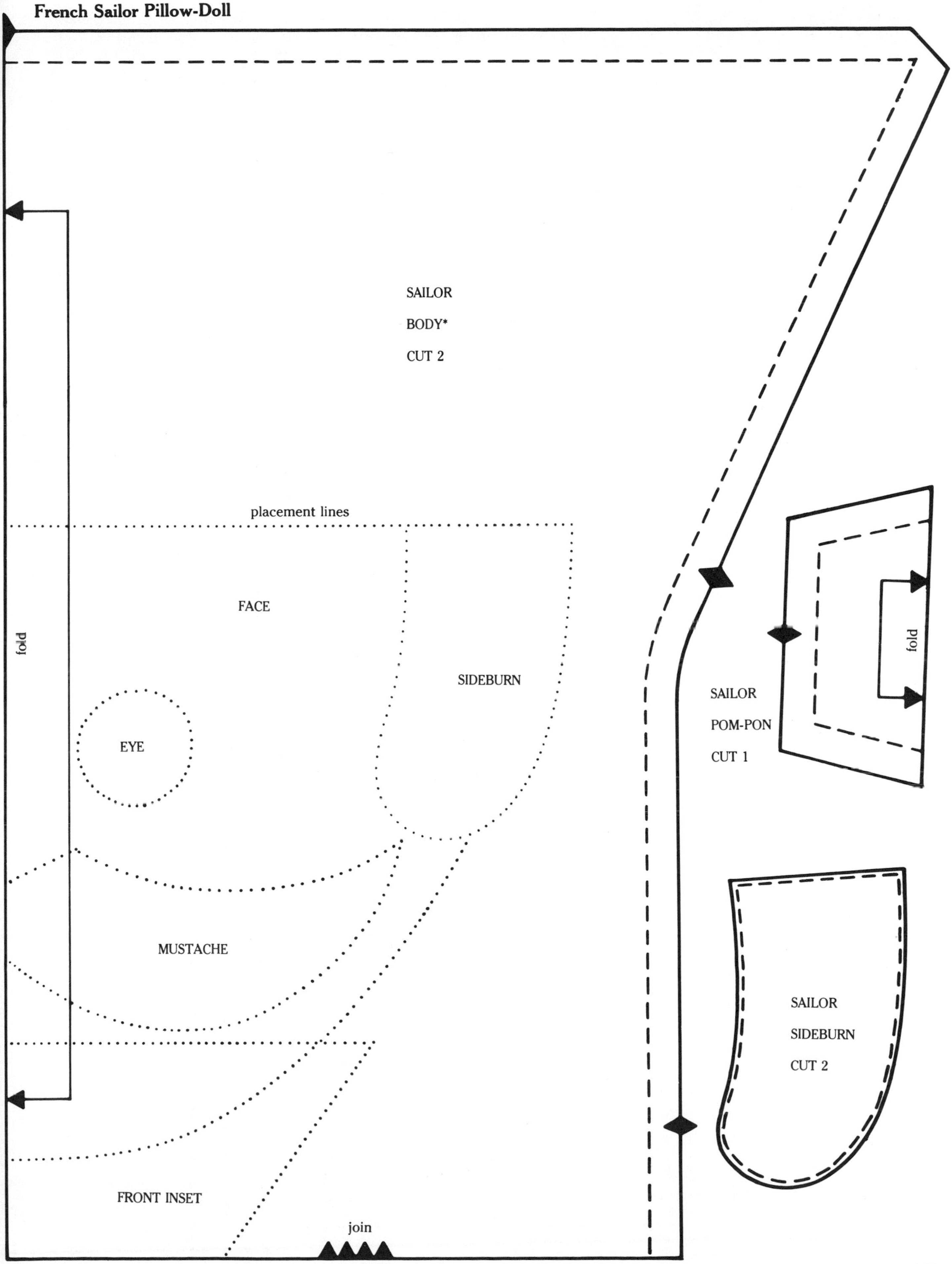

French Sailor Pillow-Doll

join
placement line
INSET
SAILOR
BODY*
CUT 2
SAILOR
BOOT
CUT 2
fold
SAILOR
HATBAND
CUT 1
fold

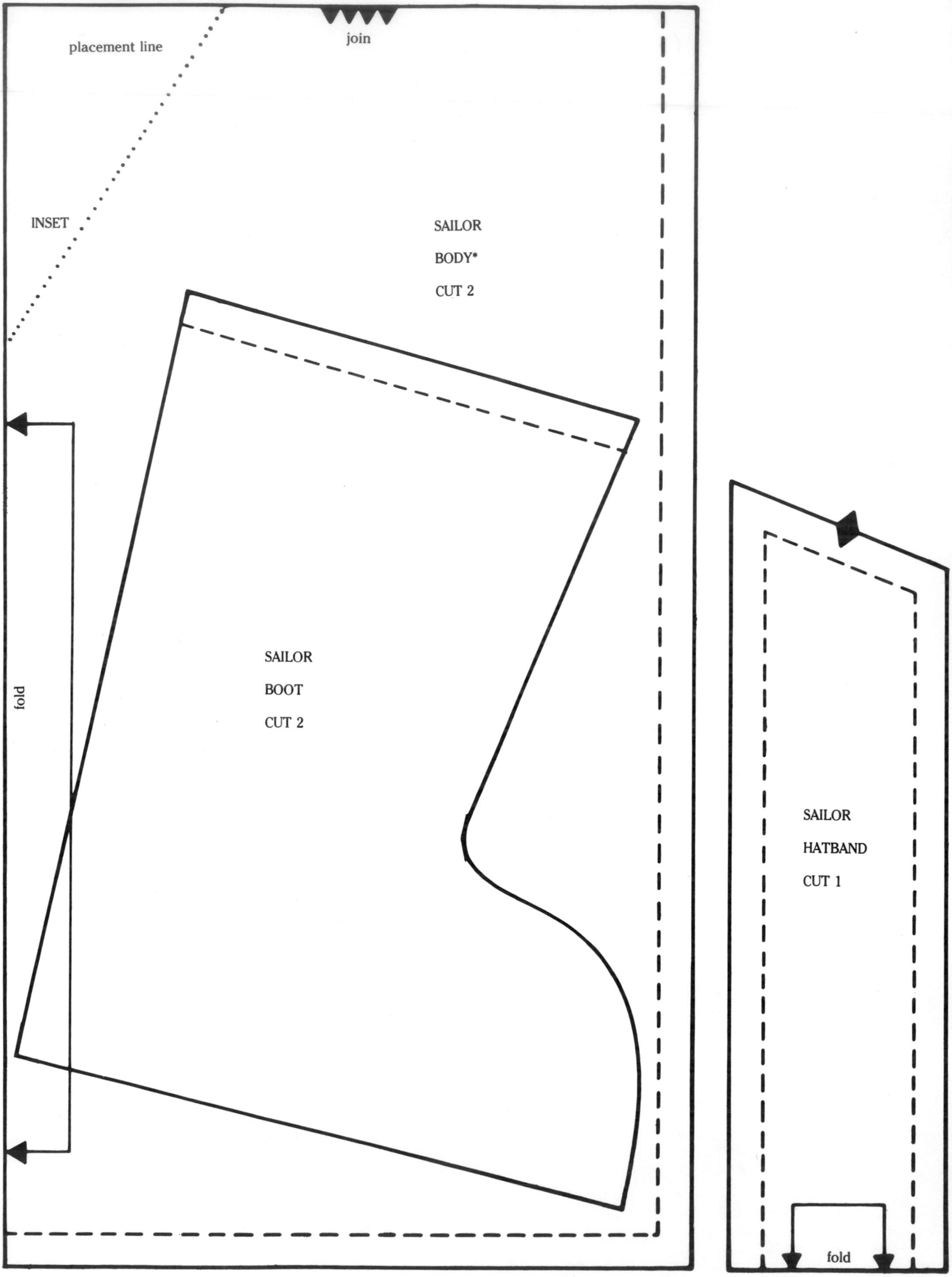

French Sailor Pillow-Doll

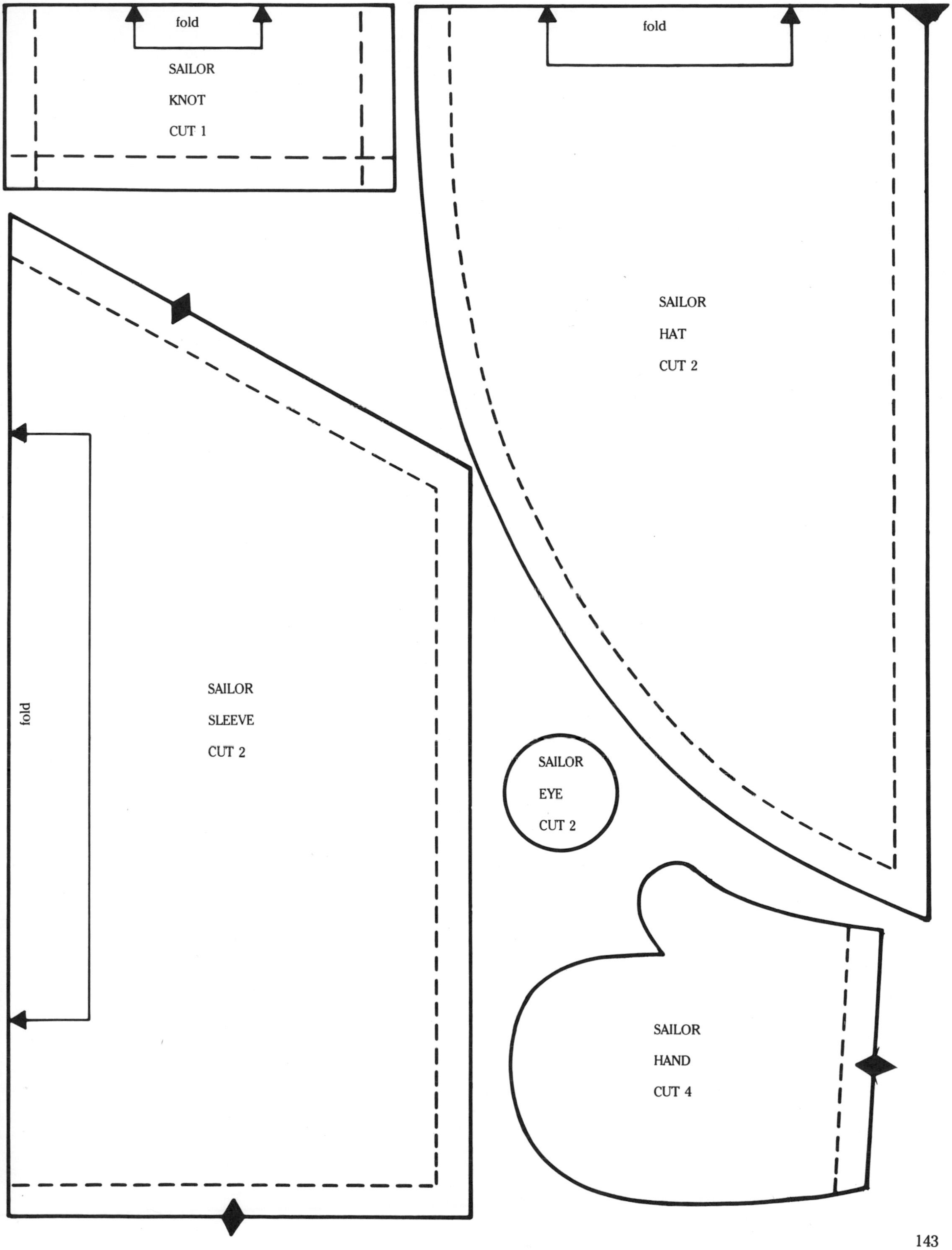

fold

SAILOR
KNOT
CUT 1

fold

SAILOR
HAT
CUT 2

SAILOR
SLEEVE
CUT 2

fold

SAILOR
EYE
CUT 2

SAILOR
HAND
CUT 4

Index